Short-Cut Quilts

60 Patterns for Creating Quilts From 5" Squares

by Doreen Cronkite Burbank

Leman Publications Inc.

For Alan, who makes everything possible.

Acknowledgments

To Jean Hay and Gerry Molina, good friends who aid and abet all my various enthusiasms; and to the skillful and dedicated quilters who were willing to work on projects for this book: Donna Christensen, Moira Clegg, Ginny Guaraldi, Jean Hay, Pam Ludwig, Terry Maddox, Beth Meek, and Karen Senet.

Credits

Editor: Lauri L. Linch-Zadel
Technical Editor: Madalene M. Becker

Cover Design: Joyce A. Robinson
Book Design: Karen Yungkurth Gerhardt
Illustrators: Doreen Cronkite Burbank
           Heidi Eberhardt
Photographer: Mellisa Karlin Mahoney
Project Manager: Suzan Ellis
Production Manager: Dorothy M. Kaiser
Project Coordinator: Michelle M. Kucharski

If you make quilts from any of the patterns in this book, we'd love to hear from you. Please send your comments, quilt stories, and photos of your projects to:

    Lauri Linch-Zadel, Editor
    Leman Publications, Inc.
    741 Corporate Circle, Suite A
    Golden, Colorado 80401-5622

Contents

Introduction

Imagine the joy of receiving a package of quilt pieces in the mail that are already sorted by color, cut to a useful size, and ready to use! The packets of assorted fabric squares that are available today from quilt shops, fabric clubs, mail-order quilt-supply companies, and fabric stores offer that kind of thrill to quilters, both novice and experienced. I call these squares *charming*, rather than charm, because most of these packets arrive with two squares each of the same print or solid-colored fabric. These extra squares can be used for trading with friends if you prefer to be a purist, and the rest used to make a traditional "charm quilt" with each fabric used only once.

This book offers many suggestions for what to do with your 5" squares using designs created especially for them. Of course, all the quilts in this book can be made from your own accumulated fabric, and many can be adapted for using charm squares cut in other sizes, if you prefer.

Many of the block designs included here are in the quick-and-easy category. I am known among my friends as a quilter who does everything by the fastest and easiest possible way and who is a whiz at finding out how to make a block using straight seams only. I cut with a rotary cutter–without using templates whenever possible–and certainly without touching pencil to fabric. I rely on the accurate ¼" seam allowance, and I have a presser foot on my sewing machine that makes sewing that allowance accurately an easy matter. Once that is mastered, everything else just falls into place.

In the first section of the book are a few suggestions for those of you who don't want to do any cutting of the 5" squares at all. Even if you want to just sew the blocks together in rows, a little pre-planning of design and sorting of color values will lead you to make a more attractive quilt.

Most of you, however, will want to get a bit more creative and explore the full potential of the fabric squares. The second section of the book shows block designs and projects that can usually be made with just one color family of 100 precut 5" squares and the addition of background fabric.

The third section of the book shows blocks that were created to exploit the design possibilities of using contrasting precut color squares. These also sometimes require the use of a background fabric and perhaps an additional accent fabric.

Because many of the blocks use the same templates, the templates are given all together in the final section of the book. Small drawings beside some of them show how those patches should be cut from a 5" square so you get the most value out of your fabric.

Browse through the book to find an appealing quilt block, and then read about the simple cutting methods that have been devised for most of the template pieces to speed up your work. This is not a how-to-make-a-quilt book as such, though general directions are included. If you are a beginner, you also should have one of the good reference books for beginners (and all the rest of us) that takes you step by step through the entire process of quiltmaking.

Remember that there is not just one way to do *anything*. I have included some of my own observations and tips to tell you about the way I choose to work. If you do things differently, think about my shortcuts, and then do what is easiest and the most fun for you! This is *your* quilt, and it should make you feel warm and loved in the process of making it as well as in the pleasure of using it.

Doreen Cronkite Burbank

General Directions

Rules, choices, and random philosophy of quiltmaking

Quilting has very few rules that aren't broken by someone making wonderful quilts. I took my first quilting workshop many years ago, and the instructor assured us that if every stitch wasn't made by hand, it wasn't *really* a quilt–just some sort of tawdry imitation. That delayed the start of my quilting by at least five years. One of the things I discovered after I did start making quilts was that my great-grandmother had used *her* sewing machine when she could to put pieces together. I knew I was descended from the right (unintimidated) stock!

Quilting (and life) is full of choices, and you should make those that increase your comfort level. If sewing machines make you nervous and stitching by hand is a pleasant time of meditation for you, by all means make any and all quilts in your preferred style. The material in this book has tips for the machine piecer, but nothing in here prohibits hand piecing. Make the templates to use for your preferred style.

A place of your own

I hope you have a wonderful place to work and good tools to use. This will make all the difference in the pleasure you have in the process of quiltmaking. To the best of your ability, set aside a special place for sewing so that your sewing machine doesn't have to be put away before supper. Have your fabric stored in a way that makes it easy to find what you have–by color groups–and keep it neatly out of the way of your family. Even better, have it stored in such a way that you can step back and admire your treasure.

Buy a good sewing machine that is appropriate for the amount and kind of sewing you do, and change its needle frequently. Your rotary cutter should be sharp (with blade changes as often as necessary), and your cutting mat should be as large as you can use in the space you have. A good pair of sharp scissors is necessary and should be reserved for cutting fabric only. An assortment of plastic rulers will allow you to use a comfortable size for small pieces instead of trying to use your biggest ruler for everything.

Money spent on good equipment saves much time and aggravation in the long run.

The wide world of fabric

Colors are a wonderful source of pleasure to me, especially the colors of fabric. When I began working with these 5″ squares, I sorted and re-sorted them into groups of color, value, and style. I soon had the packets so mixed up that I have only a vague idea which pieces came from a particular packet. I found it handy to have an assorted charm packet on hand, even when I was working with one of the single-color packets, so that I could raid it for additional pieces and perhaps substitute some color values that worked better in my project.

I set myself a mental goal when I started this book to use only the fabrics that came in precut 5" packets and the fabrics I already had in my sewing room. This really wasn't much of a limitation because I have accumulated *a lot* of fabric.

Some of the fabrics inspired projects that I hadn't even planned to make. When I ran across a few bright and amusing pieces in a charm packet, they made me think of a child's quilt. The *Baby Blocks* design was created after I saw them. This crib quilt also led me to break my first rule about using only the fabrics I had on hand. I simply didn't have enough "cute" things with white backgrounds to make a whole crib quilt, so I bought a few bright bits of things that will probably turn up in other projects eventually. (I really *did* have the lobsters on hand. They were from a gift piece of fabric a friend had brought back from Maine. I never believed I would use it, but the lobsters were perfect for turning this crib quilt into *Mainely Baby Blocks*.) This led me to a new idea to start cutting at least two 5" squares from every piece of yardage I buy, to add to my 5" squares collection.

If you are a beginning quilter, you may have been content up to now to choose from three to seven coordinated fabrics for a quilt. I hope you will branch out into the wonderful world of scrap quilts. "Scrap" is the somewhat inaccurate name we often give to quilts that are made of multiple fabrics. Fabrics in many designs and colors give these quilts a dynamic and sparkling quality that is wonderful to work with. Scrap quilts will stretch your imagination, and they are a great place to work experimentally with colors and fabrics that might intimidate you in large quantities.

When you buy the special packets of 5" die-cut squares, much of the fabric selection has been done for you. Before you start any project, however, look through your own fabric pieces to see whether you have some that would make perfect additions to your planned quilt. You can cut two 5" squares from these as necessary to add to your selection and to make the project even more your very own.

Washing and not washing

My usual custom is to wash every fabric yardage that I buy before I store it in my sewing room for future use. Because I do not usually buy fabric to use right away or for a specific project, I do not iron it after I wash it. I remove it from the dryer while it is still damp and hang it carefully over a pants hanger to air dry as straight as possible. Then I fold it up for storage. Any ironing that needs to be done is generally minimal and is done just before I am ready to cut pieces.

It is probably best to postpone washing die-cut 5" squares until after the quilt top is quilted. By doing this, you will avoid slightly distorted shapes, and the minimal shrinkage during late washing will be "absorbed" by the quilting.

One major advantage in using precut squares (besides the absolutely yummy assortment of fabric) is the wonderful straight edges they have, all measured and ready to use. I feel that keeping these edges ready to use more than compensates for the slight risk in not pre-washing the fabric.

Read the directions that come with the packets regarding laundering and decide what you prefer to do. I did *not* pre-wash my squares. In my more than 10

years of quilting, the only American fabrics I have ever had any problem with color running were some red fabrics and a few bright yellows. In using the red squares, I have taken the precaution of using a background fabric that is not white or muslin, so that any potential bleeding problem would be minimized in any case. If you are concerned that excess dye may run from very dark or intensely colored precut fabrics, soak stacks of the same-color patches in warm-water baths until the water remains clear. Handling gently, place patches in toweling or white paper towels to dry.

Background fabrics

Most of the background fabrics I used in this book have been chosen for their watercolor effect. I like this look and I search the fabric tables, particularly the sales and bargains, to find 100-percent cottons that give this splotchy, watercolor look. Sometimes a very large print will give the effect I want when it is cut into small pieces for the background.

Like most quilters, I started my career using vanilla (white or muslin) backgrounds–pastel when I was brave! Through the years, however, following good advice from fellow quilters, I became a lot more adventurous in the choice of background fabrics. Look through the samples in this book and perhaps you will be inspired to broaden your own ideas of what a background fabric can be.

Especially look at the wall hangings made from the design *Mosaic I* and *Mosaic II*–*Cherry Vanilla* and *Blueberry Ripple*. They are the same size, and they have exactly the same pieces in them, though lights and darks are rearranged slightly. The real difference is that in *Blueberry Ripple* many light blues are used instead of the muslin background fabric in *Cherry Vanilla*. Can you see how this adds sparkle to what is essentially the same wall hanging? The red and white design is static, and the blue one is dynamic.

Making templates

Many of the patches for the blocks in this book can be cut *without* making templates if you start with 5" squares. This is the easiest method. If you need to make templates, however, use any template-making method you are comfortable with. The dashed lines indicate seam lines, and the solid lines indicate cutting lines. Be sure to mark grain lines on your templates.

When only a few pieces of a particular template need to be cut, my favorite method is to trace the template (with seam allowances) onto grid-marked freezer paper that can be ironed onto the fabric. Cut around the paper template carefully, peel it off, and press it on the next piece. (It can be used at least 16 times by my actual count!)

When I *have* to cut around a template with my rotary cutter, I use a permanent template made from thick plastic or make my own from three-ply plywood. I glue the paper templates onto thin plywood scraps and cut around the templates on the bandsaw. (Fortunately, my husband has about as many wood scraps as I have fabric ones!)

For right triangles, I often work out the math so that I can cut them as half-square or quarter-square triangles from fabric squares of the appropriate size. Measurements and directions for doing this frequently are given in the book, especially for background pieces and setting triangles for projects where the blocks are set on point.

Other triangles that contain a right angle can be cut with a plastic ruler. Tape two paper copies of the template to a ruler, one in a corner and one along the bias edge, as shown in *Fig. 1*. Starting with a square corner of the fabric, cut first the bias, then the 90° angle. To cut a reverse of the template, turn the ruler over so the paper templates are on top.

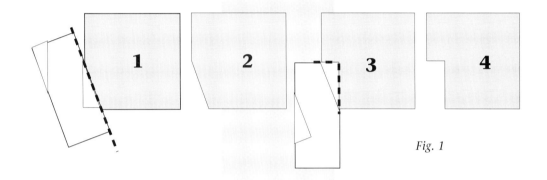

Fig. 1

Cutting the fabric

When cutting the 5" squares, you can use plastic rulers and a rotary cutter–with a *really* sharp blade, replaced if necessary before you start cutting–for nearly all the pieces. Make templates in your preferred manner for cutting the pieces from background fabric, though some speed-up hints will be given for many template pieces. Sometimes it will be faster to cut your background fabric into 5" squares and use the quick-cutting methods given for the 5" charm pieces.

Cut enough pieces for one block only (or, at most, for a group of four) and lay them out so that you can see that your colors are working well together, that your color placement is correct, and that your background fabric really works for the project. Do *not* make the mistake of cutting all your pieces for a big project first. Give yourself a chance to change your mind! Nothing is more aggravating than having cut a lot of pieces that you later decide to replace with a better choice of fabric.

If you do decide to use a precut fabric packet of 5" squares, remember that the charm pieces in most fabric packets are back to back. When you cut certain templates (such as 36 and 36-r for *Whirlagig*) it will be necessary to turn all fabrics so that the same side is up.

Marking the fabric

The only time I marked on fabric for the projects in this entire book was when

I drew with a pencil around a big coffee mug to make the center circle for *Dresden Daisy*. Marking seam lines on the fabric is something I just don't do. When you are cutting your templates correctly and machine piecing, no marking is necessary.

Some quilters have no problem with using various commercial markers, and they say they have had no trouble with them. I once won a raffle quilt on which the quilting pattern was marked with one of the chemical markers that is supposed to come out in cold water. The marking was *not* removed by several cold washings and, though it is not very noticeable, I always notice it.

As with anything, test your marker or pencil on a scrap of fabric first.

Sewing the block

Any of the quilt patterns in this book can be made by either hand or machine. The choice is completely yours to make.

If you are piecing by machine, you need to make sure to sew an accurate ¼" seam so that every piece fits together perfectly. If you don't, work to perfect this first on some sample fabric. Some ideas:

- Use a special ¼"-wide presser foot.
- Mark your foot plate with masking tape at precisely ¼".
- Adjust your needle from side to side (if your machine allows this) to see which needle setting works best. If you find that you have to change the needle setting for *any* purpose, write down the changes you have made and keep the notes on hand for when you sit down to sew again later. Do not start sewing until you can make an accurate ¼" seam!

Pressing the block

I usually press seams to one side as I go along, and I have my sewing machine and a drop-down ironing board right next to each other so that I can do this without leaving my chair. Careful pressing makes putting the next seam together easier. But remember that pressing does not mean *stretching*! Just press down, don't push from side to side as if you were ironing out wrinkles.

Generally speaking, if you press both seams toward the darker fabric, the bulk of the seams will alternate. Study your block to see which way seams should be pressed so that they can be butted up against each other with the seams facing different directions. This avoids unnecessary bulk when you get ready to quilt.

Putting the blocks together

Several kinds of settings are given in this book, but the blocks can also be used in many other kinds of settings. Some of the blocks look good when set side by side, and some really need to be set apart with plain blocks or sashing to be seen at their best.

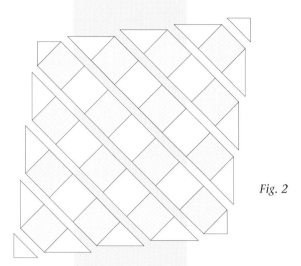

Fig. 2

A number of quilts in this book are shown with a diagonal on-point setting. The assembly drawing above (*Fig. 2*) shows how these blocks set on point are assembled into a quilt in diagonal rows.

Every time you read a quilt book or magazine, you should note settings that please you and try some of them. I have a 72"-wide piece of white felt hanging in my sewing room on which I pin finished blocks until I have an arrangement that I like. Sometimes I arrange blocks by laying them out on the floor, but only if I am going to sew them together right away–otherwise, my cat is likely to rearrange them thoroughly!

I like to use sashing and setting blocks for large projects because it is one way of making sure that the project will turn out to be really square. Measure sashing strips the size that the pattern calls for, and if you have to ease something in, you know it will square up with the other side. Sometimes just a little sashing will do, as I used in the *Whirlagig Garden* quilt. There is just enough sashing in that to give a framed effect and square up the quilt nicely.

Borders

For the same reason–being sure that the quilt is absolutely square–I cut straight borders, measuring the same on opposite sides, and sew them together with butted corners rather than mitered corners. It is easier to get a miter "off the square" than to mess up a carefully measured butted border piece. Occasionally, when I use a fancy printed border strip, I miter corners so that the design will be more attractive. Almost all of the patterns in this book (except those with pieced corner blocks) can be made with mitered corners, if you prefer.

Measurements for border strips are given with the patterns and include an extra 2½" in case your quilt blocks are too large. Always cut your borders length-wise, and always cut them first before you cut any patches. In every case, make both the left and right borders the same length and both the top and bottom borders the same length. This will help square up your quilt.

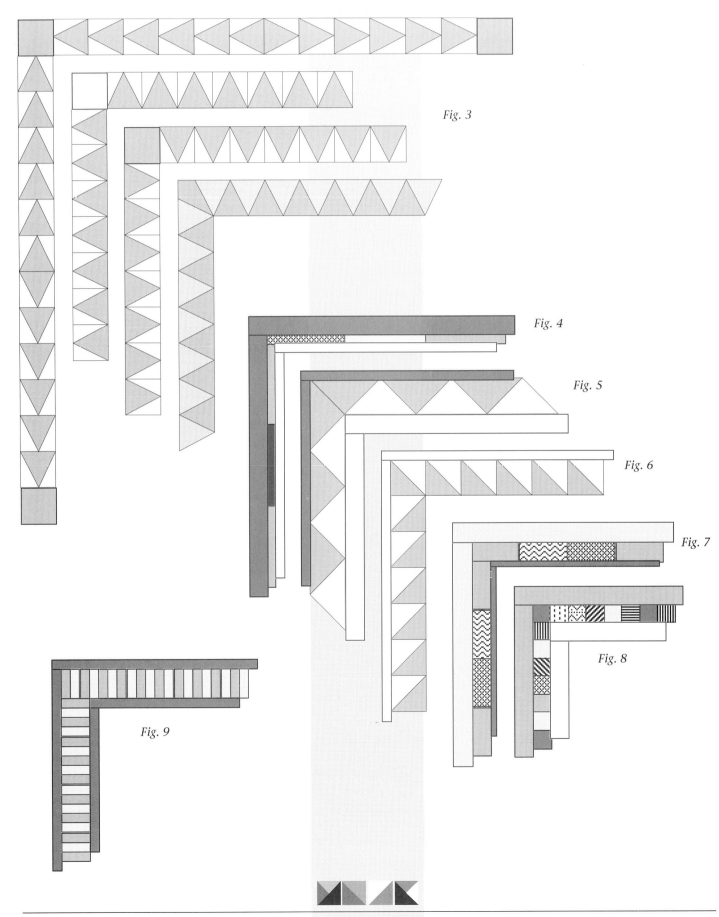

Fig. 3

Fig. 4

Fig. 5

Fig. 6

Fig. 7

Fig. 8

Fig. 9

If the sides are not exactly even, mark the border strips to the length of the shorter side with a pin, and ease in the fullness on the longer side. Always sew borders to quilt top with the border fabric on top so the feed dogs can ease in any extra fullness. You definitely do not want the border strips to be longer than the quilt top. And always wait until the border is sewn on the quilt top before you trim off any extra fabric.

I have drawn some suggestions for pieced inner borders that you may want to try if you have extra pieces to use up after cutting your 5" squares. *Fig. 3* shows four ways to create a pieced border using leftover pieces from *Templates 33, 34,* and *34-r. Fig. 4* uses leftovers from 1" strips. *Fig. 5* uses leftover pieces from *Template 5. Fig. 6* uses leftover pieces from *Templates 4, 6,* or *9. Fig. 7* uses leftover pieces from *Template 3. Fig. 8* uses leftover pieces from *Template 2.* And *Fig. 9* uses leftovers from *Templates 4, 15,* or *26.*

If the length of the pieced border needs adjusting, make adjustments in the center, not at the corners. People always look at the corners to see if they match perfectly, but they seldom check along the sides.

Layering and basting

When a quilt lining must be pieced, cut the necessary panels and remove all selvages from the sides that are to be seamed. Selvage edges can shrink over time, and you want your quilt lining relaxed.

Make the lining for the quilt about 4" larger in both length and width so that there is a margin of 2" around every edge. Cut the batting the same size. Lay them out very flat on a large table or on the floor. Mark the centers on each side of the lining and align with the centers of the sides of the quilt top. Make sure all the wrinkles are out before basting.

If you hand baste the quilt with large stitches, work from the center out to the edges. Or you can "baste" with safety pins put through all three layers. In either case, start in the middle and fasten the three layers together securely so that the quilt can be moved and handled without shifting.

Quilt as desired

You can use either hand quilting or machine quilting for any pattern in this book. All my own projects in this book are machine quilted except for *Evening Star*, which I started hand quilting in a moment of weakness because it looked so old-fashioned with its muslin background. (Maybe someday I'll even get it finished!)

Notice that no quilting patterns are given in the pattern directions. This allows you the freedom to finish the quilt any way you wish. Here are a few ideas to get you started:

■ In-the-ditch quilting–This is a line of quilting stitches (either by hand or machine) that is right next to a seam or around an appliqué patch on the side without seam allowances.

■ Outline quilting–This is quilting that outlines patches in lines that are, in

most cases, ¼" from the patch seams. This places the quilting just beyond the area where the fabric layers in the seam allowance would add extra thickness. You can use ¼"-wide masking tape as a guide.

■ Filler quilting–This includes background patterns of interlocked circles, clamshells, grids of squares or rectangles, or stipple quilting (quilting that moves in close, meandering lines to heavily quilt an area of a quilt). Sometimes you can follow the pattern of the fabric–such as a tiny vine or floral–itself. Use this type of quilting with unquilted areas so that they will be noticeably puffy by comparison.

■ Continous-line machine quilting–This is a technique using unbroken design lines that can be stitched with minimal stopping and starting. There are many good patterns of this type on the market today.

■ Cross-hatching–This is when you use parallel lines of quilting that run in two directions, forming either a grid of diamonds or a grid of squares across the entire quilt top.

■ Copying the piecing pattern–In quilt patterns set with an alternate plain block, you may wish to repeat the pieced pattern in quilting stitches on the plain block.

To hand quilt, you fasten together the layers of the quilt with running stitches. If you're a beginner, you might start off taking just one stitch at a time. After practice you'll be able to use a rocking motion to put several stitches on the needle before pulling it through. For faster results, the quilt can be machine quilted or even tied, especially if it's for a baby or a child.

Machine quilting is usually done with a walking foot that evenly feeds the quilt under the needle. Or you can also use a darning foot with the feed dogs lowered. This method allows freedom to move the quilt in any direction.

If you have never tried it, you may think that you can machine quilt as fast as you can machine piece. However, machine quilting needs to be done carefully. It is much quicker than hand quilting, but it is not something that can be rushed. Practice as much as you can on small pieces, and remember to go slowly.

I use regular weight sewing thread or a lighter machine embroidery thread in machine quilting, usually color-matched to the quilt background. When I quilt by hand, I use a good grade of quilting thread.

When the quilting is completed, baste around the outside edge of the quilt top, if necessary, and trim the batting and lining to extend ⅛" beyond the quilt top with your large ruler and rotary cutter to make an even edge.

Bind to finish

Bindings are usually the first thing to wear out on a quilt, so I almost always use a double thickness of fabric cut on the straight of the grain because I prefer the non-stretch quality of straight-grain binding. Directions here are given for straight-grain binding, but you may wish to use other binding methods on your quilts instead. Since binding must nearly always be pieced, cut the ends of the strips on the bias and piece together so that you do not have the bulk of a straight seam (*Fig. 10.*)

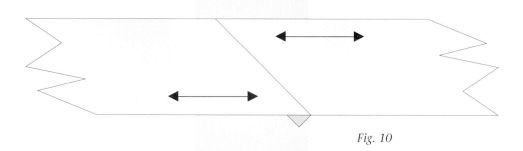

Fig. 10

First decide on the width of the binding you want to have on your quilt. If your blocks go all the way to the edge of the quilt, you must plan a ¼" binding because that is all the seam allowance that you will have. With added borders you will gain flexibility. (When I make a large quilt, I almost always use outer borders, and I usually plan for a ⅜" binding on a large quilt.)

To figure the width of your strips for double binding, multiply the width you want (⅜") times three (nine-eighths or 1⅛") and add ⅛" inch (to make 1¼"). Multiply this by two (2½"). Cut your binding strips 2½" wide and press them in half.

If you were paying attention above, you may well ask what happens to that extra ⅛" that I added in? I'm not sure why, but it always seems to disappear in the various foldings and thicknesses of the binding. If you don't have it, the binding seems to come out narrower than planned. If your binding seems thin, stuff it with a narrow strip of batting.

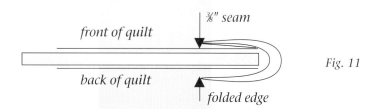

front of quilt

⅜" seam

back of quilt

folded edge

Fig. 11

Sew the side of the binding with the raw edges to the outside edge of the quilt top, using a walking foot so that nothing is stretched. Start sewing the binding in the center of one side of the quilt.

To turn a corner with the binding, sew the binding to the quilt top to ⅜" from the edge, backstitch a few stitches, and then cut your threads and remove from the sewing machine needle. Turn the binding so that the fold is even with the sewn edge, and begin sewing the second side ⅜" from the top (*Fig. 12*). The ends of

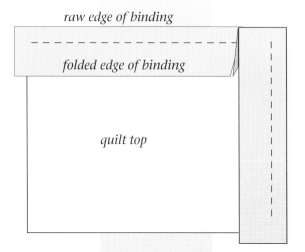

raw edge of binding

folded edge of binding

quilt top

Fig. 12

the two seams should touch. When you get around to where you started, trim the binding so that the two ends can be sewn together with a bias seam, and finish sewing.

Turn the folded edge to the back, tuck the corner in like a mitered corner, and hand sew the folded edge along the seam line by hand.

And last but not least

Make a label with the quilt's name, your name, town, and the date so that the quilt will always be identified with you–and enjoy!

Diagonal Stripe

Diagonal Stripe pattern (page 32), 78½" x 92", machine pieced by the author;
machine quilted with commercial quilting machine by Patricia Mamacos,
Newbury, Massachusetts, 1993. This quilt was made to demonstrate the
orderly arrangement of color and value that makes a very simple quilt more
interesting. Because the piecing was so plain, the author sent it out to be
commercially quilted with a fairly elaborate curved design.

Crossed Anvils

Variation of the Anvil pattern (page 42), 43" x 43", machine pieced and hand
quilted by Donna Christensen, Lincoln, Nebraska, 1994.
Green patches are used in this wall hanging to make a star-like
interpretation of the traditional Anvil block.

Mainely Baby Blocks

Baby Blocks pattern (page 44), 40" x 52½", machine pieced and machine quilted by the author, 1993. Terry Maddox distributed a quarter yard of lobster fabric to each of the Windham quilters, and some of it ended up in this baby quilt, hence the title. The other "block top" fabrics were chosen from bright patterns on white that would appeal to a young child.

Sky Blocks

Baby Blocks pattern (page 46), 29" x 32", machine pieced and machine quilted by the author, 1993. This small wall hanging was made as a demonstration piece to show how each "surface" of each block could be made from a different fabric. Since it seemed to float on the dark background, the sky and rainbow fabric borders seemed appropriate.

Autumn Harvest

Basket pattern (page 48), 47" x 47", machine pieced and hand quilted by
Karen Senet, Londonderry, New Hampshire, 1994. Karen chose an all-solid
fabric palette in Amish-inspired colors for her autumn baskets. The quilting
pattern of grapes and grape leaves is done in metallic thread on the black
corner and setting triangles. Karen decided against adding borders to her quilt.

Daisy, Daisy

Dresden Daisy pattern (page 52), 35" x 35", machine pieced and machine quilted by the author, 1993. This pattern was completely inspired by the act of cutting the charm squares into rectangular halves and then wondering what to do with them. The 1930s look of the pattern led to the blanket stitch machine appliqué.

Fantutti

Dresden Fan pattern (page 55), 36" x 36", machine pieced and machine quilted by Terry Maddox, Pelham, New Hampshire, 1994. Terry trimmed this gathered version of the traditional fan pattern with eyelet lace. Her usual painstaking work makes this simple wall hanging a real treat.

Stardusk

Variation of the Eccentric Star pattern (page 56), 64" x 85", machine pieced and machine quilted by Virginia L. Guaraldi, Londonderry, New Hampshire, 1994. Machine quilted quotes around the narrow border read: "Light fades stars appear, Evening angels gather here. At dusk, truth be told, outdoors is better than in...the crickets, you know."

Ginny works well with the graduated colors depicting stars appearing at dusk. She chose to set five blocks side by side in six rows, rather than alternating them with plain blocks as shown in the pattern.

Evening in America

Evening Star pattern (page 60), 84" x 104", machine pieced and hand and
machine quilted by the author, 1994. The scraps in this quilt were
accumulated during an extensive over-buying of red and navy blue prints in
the past, and all came from the author's scrap collection. The color scheme
dictated a patriotic title, and the old-fashioned look
of the muslin background seemed to cry out for hand quilting.

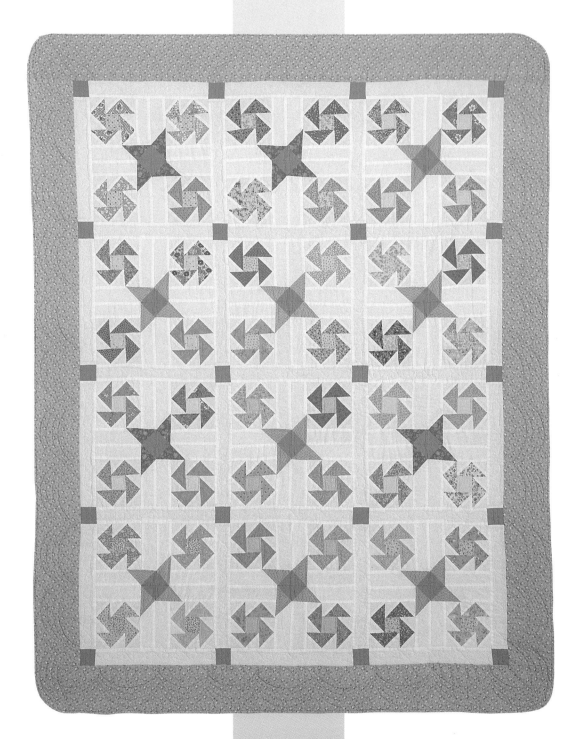

Sweet Nothing

Variation of the Mayflower pattern (page 64), 61" x 75½", machine pieced and hand quilted by Pam Ludwig, Windham, New Hampshire, 1994. Pam's usual color choices are much more vivid, but she felt this quilt called for a more muted palette. Since it contained "sweet" pastel colors that she seldom uses, she called it a "sweet nothing."
Pam made the quilt smaller by setting the quilt in four rows of three rather than the five rows of four called for in the pattern.

No-Cut Quilts

Sewing 5″ squares of fabric randomly together is the easiest way to use them to make a quilt. This type of quilt, however, can be boring or interesting, depending on the care you take in planning the arrangement of the pieces.

When planning a quilt project using 5″ squares, remember that a ¼″ seam allowance is necessary on all sides, making the finished size 4½″ square (*Template 1* on page 135). This is a somewhat larger square than quilters generally use, but with a little forethought the pieces can be very attractively arranged without any further cutting.

Several options in arrangement and placement of the pieces are given in this section, from a color-shading treatment to a checkerboard design. The best tip to remember is to practice arranging and placing your squares until you get an arrangement that's pleasing to you!

Color Shading

One option in arrangement and placement of the squares involves dividing the 5" pieces into color values–lights, mediums, and darks. These types of quilts are called Color Shading quilts.

The effect will generally be more pleasing in putting together many different fabrics if some order is imposed on them. In each of the illustrations of *Color Shading I* and *Color Shading II*, the darker squares are in the center. Sometimes if the center is the lightest, it can look as if there is a hole in the center of the quilt. If you want to contain the lighter colors on the outside, add a dark border around the quilt.

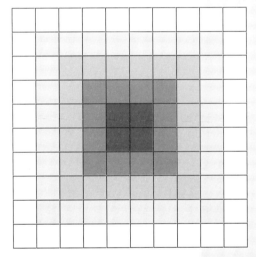

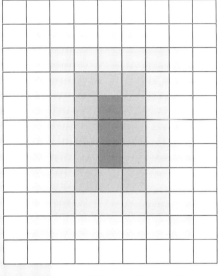

Color Shading I

Block size: 4½"

Quilt size: 45" x 45"

Skill level: beginner

Color Shading II

Block size: 4½"

Quilt size: 40½" x 49½"

Skill level: beginner

Color Shading I–*100 squares make a 45" x 45" quilt when set 10 x 10.*

Color Shading II–*99 squares make a 40½" x 49½" quilt when set 9 x 11.*

Color Shading III–*100 squares sorted dark to light and set 10 x 10 make a 45" x 45" quilt.*

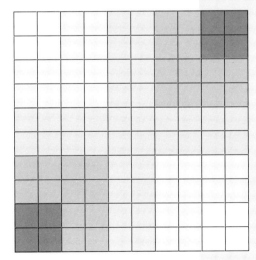

Color Shading III

Block size: 4½"

Quilt size: 45" x 45"

Skill level: beginner

Materials

(40" fabric)

■ **5" Squares**
100 pieces

■ **Binding**
⅜ yard
　2½" x 5½ yards

■ **Lining**
2¾ yards
　2 panels 25" x 49"

■ **Batting**
49" x 49"

Color Shading III shows an arrangement of the pieces that has darks in opposite corners, lights in opposite corners, and shading to mediums in the center. All these quilts are fairly small because only 100 squares are used. You can keep adding 5" squares to make a larger quilt.

For each project use 100 of the 5" squares in a single color family. No cutting is required. Borders may be added to the project after the quilt top is completed.

Assembly

1. Arrange the pieces in a manner that is pretty to you. Do not hesitate to remove any pieces that do not please you and replace with other pieces that are more to your liking.

2. Pin horizontal rows together in order, and pick up one row at a time to sew the seams. (You may lose track of which row is which if you work with too many rows at a time.) Or you can pin a small piece of paper indicating the row number and the left side as a reminder.

3. Press the seams in the top row so that all are folded the same way. Press the seams in the second row in the opposite direction so the seams will fit nicely together. Continue down the rows until the top is completed. This quilt will be most attractive when careful attention is paid to matching the seams at the corners of the blocks.

4. If you wish to make this project bigger, add borders to make a crib or lap quilt.

5. Baste together top, batting, and lining. Quilt as desired. Bind to finish.

Needle **Note**

Try this exercise in color selection: The next time you buy a packet of 100 die-cut 5" print squares in a single color family, sort all the pieces in three piles–lights, mediums, and darks. Arrange the pieces on the floor and then step back from your arrangement to see which squares seem to "stick out" as if they are in the wrong place. Rearrange until you are satisfied with the gradation of color.

Checkerboard

In *Checkerboard I*, 97 squares of the same color and pattern are alternated with 98 squares in random colors and patterns. With borders added, this quilt could be used as a quilt for a twin-size bed.

Checkerboard II uses alternating background fabric pieces and the color-shading arrangement from dark to light.

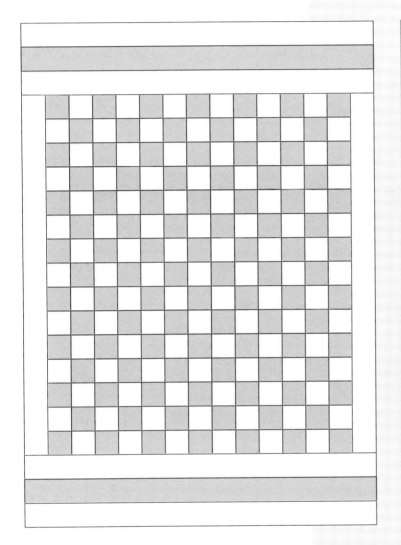

Checkerboard I quilt
Block size: 4½"
Quilt size: 67½" x 94½"
Set 13 x 15
Skill level: beginner

Checkerboard II quilt
Block size: 4½"
Quilt size: 58½" x 85½"
Set 11 x 17
Skill level: beginner

Materials
(40" fabric)

Checkerboard I
■ **5" Squares**
98 pieces

■ **Background and binding**
4 yards
97 squares 5" x 5"
(*Template 1*)
6 strips 5" x 70"
(cut lengthwise)
binding strips
(2½" x 9½ yards)

■ **Dark border strips**
2⅛ yards
2 strips 5" x 70"

■ **Lining**
5½ yards
2 panels 37" x 99"

■ **Batting**
72" x 99"

Checkerboard II
■ **5" Squares**
93 pieces

■ **Background fabric**
2 yards
94 squares 5" x 5"

■ **Border and binding**
2⅓ yards
2 strips 5" x 79" for sides
2 strips 5" x 61" for
top and bottom
binding strips
(2½" x 8½ yards)

■ **Lining**
5¼ yards
2 panels 32" x 90"

■ **Batting**
63" x 90"

Checkerboard I Assembly

1. Note that alternate rows begin and end with either the background fabric squares or the 5" charm squares. You may wish to lay out one or several horizontal rows of squares at a time. Pin these horizontal rows together and sew seams.

2. When all your horizontal rows are sewn, lay them out on the floor and pick up the top 2 rows to sew together. Press all the seams in the top row in one direction and the seams in the second row in the opposite direction. This allows seams to be butted together smoothly and reduces bulk. As you add rows, check to see which direction the seams should be pressed.

3. Sew a border strip cut from the background fabric to either side of the center panel; trim to fit.

4. Sew a border strip cut from the background fabric to either side of a dark border strip. Sew this border row to top of quilt; trim to fit. Repeat for the bottom border.

5. Baste together top, batting, and lining. Quilt as desired. Bind to finish.

Checkerboard II Assembly

1. Lay out your 5" charm squares in a color-shading fashion (see quilt diagram). When you have a pleasing arrangement, alternate with background fabric squares. Note that rows begin and end with 5" charm squares and background squares alternately.

2. Pin these horizontal rows together and sew seams. When all your horizontal rows are together, lay them out on the floor and pick up the top two rows to sew together. Press all the seams in the top row in one direction and the seams in the second row in the opposite direction. This allows seams to be butted together smoothly and reduces bulk. As you add rows, check to see which direction the seams should be pressed.

3. Add side borders to either side of center panel; trim to fit. Add top and bottom borders; trim to fit.

4. Baste together top, batting, and lining. Quilt as desired. Bind to finish.

Checkerboard III

Checkerboard III uses two different color families, set alternately. The colors must provide sufficient contrast with each other, such as a combination of whites with a dark color such as blue. Consider the possibilities of shading this quilt from dark at the center to light at the outer edges.

Checkerboard III quilt

Block size: 4½"
Quilt size: 76½" x 85½"
Set 13 x 15
Skill level: beginner

Materials

(40" fabric)

■ *5" Squares*
(color 1, indicated by dark)
97 pieces

■ *5" Squares*
(color 2, indicated by light)
98 pieces

■ *Inner border*
2⅛ yards
   4 strips 5" x 70"

■ *Outer border and binding*
2⅓ yards
   4 strips 5" x 79"
   binding strips
      (2½" x 9½ yards)

■ *Lining*
6¾ yards
   3 panels 31" x 81"

■ *Batting*
81" x 90"

Assembly

1. You may wish to lay out one or several horizontal rows of squares at a time. Pin these horizontal rows together and sew seams.

2. When you have sewn all your horizontal rows, lay them out on the floor and pick up the top 2 rows to sew together. Press all the seams in the top row in one direction and the seams in the second row in the opposite direction. This allows seams to be butted together smoothly and reduces bulk. As you add rows, check to see which direction the seams should be pressed.

3. If you would like to make this quilt 9" longer (76½" x 94½"), cut 13 additional 5" squares of color 1 and 13 additional 5" squares of color 2 to make 2 more horizontal rows.

4. Add side borders to either side of quilt center; trim to fit. Add top and bottom borders; trim to fit.

5. Baste together top, batting, and lining. Quilt as desired. Bind to finish.

Diagonal Stripe

Two different color families of prints could also be set in wide diagonal rows as shown in *Diagonal Stripe*. Two color families sorted into lights and darks will make a strong diagonal design. The bands of colored squares are separated by 5″ squares of accent fabric. This makes the separation of colors more apparent and also increases the size of the quilt top.

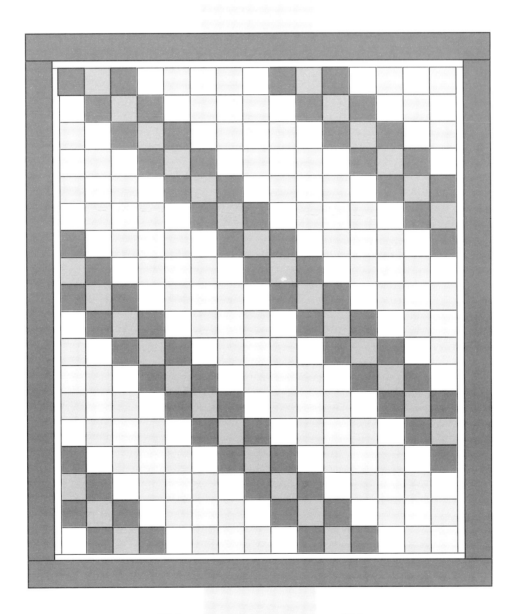

Diagonal Stripe quilt

Block size: 4½″
Quilt size: 78½″ x 92″
Set 15 x 18
Skill level: beginner

Materials

(40" fabric)

■ *5" Squares*
(color 1, indicated by dark)
102 pieces

■ *5" Squares*
(color 2, indicated by light)
100 pieces

■ *Accent squares and inner border*
2½ yards
   68 squares 5" x 5" (*Template 1*)
   2 strips 1½" x 83½"
      for sides
   2 strips 1½" x 72"
      for top and bottom

■ *Outer border and binding*
2½ yards
   2 strips 5" x 85½"
      for sides
   2 strips 5" x 81"
      for top and bottom
   binding strips
      (2½" x 10 yards)

■ *Lining*
7 yards
   3 panels 33" x 83"

■ *Batting*
83" x 96"

Assembly

1. Sort 2 color families (color 1 and color 2) separately into light and dark piles so you have 4 piles. From each color group, about two-thirds should be designated as dark.

2. As the colors proceed across the horizontal rows, place the dark color 1s on either side of the light colors 1s, and the dark color 2s on either side of the light color 2s. Use an accent block to separate a color 1 group of 3 from the color 2 group of 3.

3. Make 18 horizontal rows, following the color arrangement in the quilt diagram.

4. Add inner side borders to either side of center panel; trim to fit. Add inner top and bottom borders; trim to fit. Add outer side borders; trim to fit. Add outer top and bottom borders; trim to fit.

5. Baste together top, batting, and lining. Quilt as desired. Bind to finish.

Boston Common

Boston Common quilt shows the squares set on the diagonal. Two color families make wide bands of alternating colors. Fill-in triangles are required around the outside of the quilt to square it up. These can be cut from a blending background fabric using a no-template method or use *Templates 24* and *25* (page 142-143.) Adding rows of 5″ squares cut from background fabric between the bands of colored squares (as done diagonally in *Diagonal Stripe*) will make a larger quilt.

Boston Common quilt
Block size 4½″
Quilt size: 71⅜″ x 86″
Set 10 x 11 (on point)
Skill level: beginner

Materials

(40" fabric)

■ **5" Squares**
(color 1, indicated by dark)
108 pieces

■ **5" Squares**
(color 2, indicated by light)
92 pieces

■ **Setting triangles**
¾ yard

4 of *Template 24*
for the corners

38 of *Template 25* for setting
triangles around sides

■ **Inner border and binding**
2⅛ yards

2 strips 2½" x 72½"
for sides

2 strips 4½" x 70⅛"
for top and bottom

binding
(2½" x 9¼ yards)

■ **Outer border**
2⅓ yards

2 strips 2½" x 80½"
for sides

2 strips 4½" x 74⅛"
for top and bottom

■ **Lining**
5 yards

2 panels 38" x 90"

■ **Batting**
76" x 90"

Assembly

1. Sort out squares in 2 color families as described in the directions for *Diagonal Stripe* (page 33), with approximately a third of each group designated as dark.

2. Arrange these squares on a sheet on the floor, following the arrangement in the quilt drawing. Pin pieces into place in case you may be interrupted or need to pick up the sheet.

3. Cut the setting triangles for the sides and corners from background fabric. When cutting these pieces, be aware of the grain line because the outside edge of the quilt should be entirely on the straight of the grain.

4. Pin pieces together in diagonal rows as described in the general directions about quilts with blocks that are set on point (page 11). Make 24 rows. Sew rows together, following quilt diagram.

5. Add inner side borders to either side of center panel; trim to fit. Add inner top and bottom borders; trim to fit. Add outer side borders; trim to fit. Add outer top and bottom borders; trim to fit.

6. Baste together top, batting, and lining. Quilt as desired. Bind to finish.

Needle **Note**

For no-template cutting of Templates *24 and 25, cut two 4⅞" squares diagonally once from corner to corner to make half-square triangles for the four corner pieces. Cut ten 7¾" squares diagonally twice from corner to corner to make 38 quarter-square triangles for the sides of the quilt.*

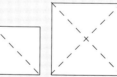

Cutting diagram for half-square triangles (left) and quarter-square triangles (right).

Large Patch Quilts

Use 5" charm squares in either two color values, light and dark, or two different color families to make the Nine Patch or Five Patch and setting squares for these quilts. Arrange these with sashing of the same width.

Large Nine Patch quilt
Block size: 13½"
Quilt size: 76½" x 94½"
Set 4 x 5
Skill level: beginner

Large Five Patch quilt
Block size: 22½"
Quilt size: 85½" x 112½"
Set 3 x 4
Skill level: beginner

Materials
(40" fabric)

Large Nine Patch
■ *5" Squares*

210 pieces (includes 30 for setting squares)

■ *Sashing and binding*
3¾ yards

    49 sashing strips
        cut 5" x 14"
    binding strips
        (2½" x 10 yards)

■ *Lining*
5⅝ yards

    2 panels 40" x 99"

■ *Batting*
80" x 99"

Large Five Patch
■ *5" Squares*
300 pieces

■ *Setting squares*
½ yard

    20 pieces 5" x 5"
        (*Template 1*)

■ *Sashing and binding*
3½ yards

    31 sashing strips 5" x 23"
    binding strips
        (2½" x 11½ yards)

■ *Lining*
7⅝ yards

    3 panels 90" x 39"

■ *Batting*
90" x 117"

Large Nine Patch Assembly

1. Alternate light and dark squares to make a simple Nine Patch block, sewing horizontal rows first and then sewing groups of 3 together. Make 20 blocks. Half the blocks should have darks on the outer corners and center, and the other half should have lights on the outer corners and center.

2. From background fabric, cut 7 strips 14"-wide. Cut these into 5" wide pieces to make 49 sashing strips 5" x 14".

3. Join 4 blocks alternately with 5 sashing strips to make a block row. Make 5 block rows.

4. Join 5 setting squares alternately with 4 sashing strips to make a sash row. Make 6 sash rows. Join block rows and sash rows, alternating types.

5. Baste together top, batting, and lining. Quilt as desired. Bind to finish.

Large Five Patch Assembly

1. Divide 300 of the 5" squares into lights and darks. Sew 5 squares together, alternating darks and lights, in horizontal rows, and then assemble block by sewing 5 rows together. Make 12 blocks.

2. Cut 20 of the 5" squares for the setting squares.

3. From a background fabric, cut 31 sashing strips 5" x 23".

4. Join 3 blocks alternately with 4 sashing strips to make a block row. Make 4 block rows.

5. Join 4 setting squares alternately with 3 sashing strips to make a sash row. Join block rows and sash rows, alternating types.

6. Baste together top, batting, and lining. Quilt as desired. Bind to finish.

Large Four Patch Quilts

Arranging the pieces in groups to make large blocks offers other possibilities for using the pieces in no-cut quilts. The *Large Four Patch* block is 9″ square and uses four pieces, two squares from each of two contrasting color families.

Large Four Patch quilt

Block size: 9″

Quilt size: 90″ x 108″

Set 9 x 11

Skill level: beginner

Large Diagonal Four Patch quilt

Block size: 9″

Quilt size: 85½″ x 111″

Set 6 x 8 (on point)

Skill level: beginner

Directions for this quilt are on page 40.

Materials

(40″ fabric)

Large Four Patch
■ *5″ Squares* (color 1)
100 pieces

■ *5″ Squares* (color 2)
100 pieces

■ *Background fabric*
3⅝ yards
49 squares 9½″ x 9½″

■ *Borders and binding*
3 yards
2 strips 5″ x 101½″
  for sides
2 strips 5″ x 92½″
  for top and bottom
binding strips
  (2½″ x 11½ yards)

■ *Lining*
8 yards
3 panels 38″ x 94″

■ *Batting*
94″ x 112″

Large Four Patch Assembly

1. Make each Four Patch block using 4 of the 5″ squares, 2 from each color family. 200 squares will make 50 blocks, as shown in the quilt diagram.

2. Cut 49 squares 9½″ x 9½″ from background fabric.

3. Make 6 rows, alternating 5 Four Patch blocks with 4 background blocks. Make 5 rows, alternating 5 background blocks with 4 Four Patch blocks. Sew rows together, alternating between types, following the quilt diagram.

4. Add side borders to either side of the center panel; trim to fit. Add top and bottom borders; trim to fit.

5. Baste together top, batting, and lining. Quilt as desired. Bind to finish.

Needle **Note**

Alternating plain squares with pieced blocks provides large areas for fancy quilting motifs. The quilting can do much to keep the design in motion. If you will be quilting special motifs in the alternating squares, choose a solid-color fabric to let the quilting stitches show; a print will disguise the quilting or make it disappear.

Materials

(40" fabric)

Large Diagonal Four Patch

■ **5" Squares** (color 1)
96 pieces

■ **5" Squares** (color 2)
96 pieces

■ **Background fabric**
3¾ yards

35 squares 9½" x 9½"

6 squares 14" x 14"
(Cut each diagonally both
ways to make 24
quarter-square triangles
with straight of grain on
long edge.)

2 squares 7¼" x 7¼"
(Cut each diagonally one
way to make 4 half-square
triangles for the corners.)

■ **Borders**
3⅛ yards

2 strips 4½" x 105½"
for sides

2 strips 4½" x 88"
for top and bottom

■ **Binding**
1 yard
(2½" x 11⅜ yards)

■ **Lining**
7½ yards
3 panels 39" x 89½"

■ **Batting**
89½" x 115"

Large Diagonal Four Patch Assembly

1. Make 48 Four Patch blocks, using 4 of the 5" squares, 2 from each color family.

2. Cut background fabric into alternate plain blocks and setting triangles, following directions in the materials box.

3. Assemble in diagonal rows as shown in the general directions for quilts set on point. Make 13 rows.

4. Add inner side borders to either side of the center panel; trim to fit. Add inner top and bottom borders; trim to fit. Add outer side borders; trim to fit. Add outer top and bottom borders; trim to fit.

5. Baste together top, batting, and lining. Quilt as desired. Bind to finish.

Needle **Note**

If you plan an elaborate quilting motif to fill the plain blocks, press seams toward the pieced blocks so that you can quilt close to the seam line and the seam allowances won't show through the patches.

Quick-Cut Quilts

Now that you've had some practice grouping your 5″ squares into effective color arrangements, try cutting them up into different shapes for a greater variety of patterns. This section shows you how to use the handy templates (pages 135-144) and fast-cut methods to get your patches ready quickly and simply.

Many of these patterns require only one color family of squares plus a background fabric. And remember, if you have leftover pieces from any quilt project, don't throw them away! If you've cut carefully, many of the spare patches can be saved and used in other quilt projects or even in pieced borders (page 12).

Anvil

This traditional block can be made from one color family or it can be made from several. If a second color is added, make the squares (*Template 2*) from the background accent color. Or to unify the quilt even further, make all the *Template 2* pieces from the same accent fabric.

Anvil can make a nice overall design, but it's also particularly nice when the blocks are separated by sashing. In the Crossed Anvils quilt, the block makes a secondary pattern of small stars inside large ones.

Crossed Anvils quilt

Block size: 8″
Quilt size: 82″ x 100″
Set 4 x 5
Skill level: beginner/intermediate

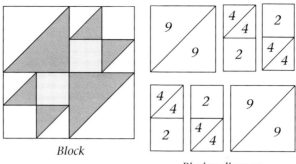

Block

Piecing diagram

Materials
(40" fabric)

■ 5" Squares
200 pieces
- 160 of *Template 9*
- 320 of *Template 4*
- 160 of *Template 2*

■ Setting squares
¼ yard
- 30 of *Template 2**

■ Background fabric
5⅝ yards
- 160 of *Template 9*
- 320 of *Template 4*
- 160 of *Template 2*
  (or you may use 200-5"
  squares for quick-cutting
  of your *Templates 9, 4,
  and 2.*)
- 49 sashing strips
  2½" x 16½"

■ Borders and binding
2⅞ yards
- 2 strips 4½" x 94½"
  for sides
- 2 strips 4½" x 84½"
  for top and bottom
- binding strips
  (2½" x 10½ yards)

■ Lining
7¼ yards
- 3 panels 35" x 86"

■ Batting
86" x 104"

Assembly

1. Cut block patches and 30 setting squares as directed.*

2. From background fabric, cut sashing strips first, then *Templates 2, 4,* and *9* as directed.

3. Make 80 Anvil blocks following the block drawing and piecing diagram. Arrange in 20 groups of 4, rotating each as shown in the quilt diagram to make 20 large units.

4. Join 4 units alternately with 5 sashing strips to make a unit row. Make 5 unit rows.

5. Join 5 setting squares alternately with 4 sashing strips to make a sash row. Make 6 sash rows. Join unit rows and sash rows, alternating types.

6. Baste together top, batting, and lining. Quilt as desired. Bind to finish.

Needle **Note**

* If using a single accent color for Template 2 patches in the block and for the setting squares, buy 1½ yards of the background fabric, and cut 190 of Template 2, eliminating the cutting of Template 2 block patches from 5" squares described in the materials list. In this case, only 160 5" squares will be required.

Baby Blocks

No cutting is required for the center piece (*Template 1*) of Baby Blocks and, unlike most patterns with this name, you do not have to inset any seams, which can make sewing difficult for beginners. Note that because of the grain line, *Template 25* cannot be cut from a 5" square.

Choose fabrics for the shading triangles that will not clearly show seam lines when cut and sewed back together. You can use two different fabrics for the medium triangles as I did, but this is not necessary. Yardage is given for all medium triangles so that they can be cut from the same fabric.

This block would also be charming in a lap size quilt with flowers in the center blocks and pastels for the shading triangles.

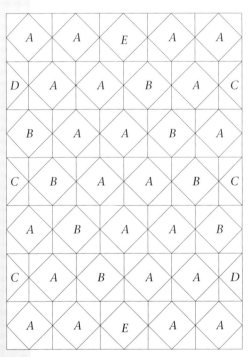

Quilt diagram

Mainely Baby Blocks

Block size: 6⅜"
Quilt size: 40" x 52½"
Set 5 x 7
Skill level: beginner

Materials

(40" fabric)

 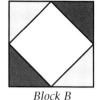

Piecing diagrams

Block A   Block B   Block C   Block D   Block E

■ **5" Squares**

(block tops, indicated by white)

32 pieces

32 of *Template 1*

■ **Similar fabric**

(indicated by white)

¼ yard

6 of *Template 25**
for half-block tops

■ **Dark shading, inner border, and binding**

1½ yards

70 of *Template 24***
2 strips 1½" x 47"
for sides
2 strips 1½" x 36½"
for top and bottom
binding strips
(2½" x 5⅝ yards)

■ **Medium shading**

½ yard

70 of *Template 24***
(cut only 50 if using optional light shading)

■ **Light shading**

¼ yard (optional)**

20 of *Template 24*

■ **Outer border**

1½ yards

2 border strips
3½" x 49" for sides
2 border strips
3½" x 42½"
for top and bottom

■ **Lining**

2½ yards

2 panels 29" x 44"

■ **Batting**

44" x 57"

Assembly

1. *Template 1* is a 5" square and requires no cutting. You'll need 32 of these for the block tops. Cut 6 *Template 25* pieces for Block C and Block D from a fabric that is the same or similar to the pieces you have chosen to use for *Template 1*.

2. Cut inner border strips from dark fabric before cutting 70 *Template 24* pieces.

3. Cut 70 *Template 24* pieces from medium fabric. (If using the optional light shading, cut 20 from light fabric and 50 from medium fabric.)

4. Following the block drawings and piecing diagrams, make 32 of Block A, 6 of Block C, and eliminate Blocks B, D, and E if using only dark and medium fabrics. (To use optional light shading, make 22 of Block A, 8 of Block B, 4 of Block C, 2 of Block D, and 2 of Block E, following the block drawings and piecing diagrams.)

5. Assemble as shown in the quilt diagram.

6. Add inner side borders to either side of center panel; trim to fit. Add inner top and bottom borders; trim to fit. Add outer side borders; trim to fit. Add outer top and bottom borders; trim to fit.

7. Baste together top, batting, and lining. Quilt as desired. Bind to finish.

Needle **Note**

**For no-template cutting, cut a 7¾" square diagonally twice from opposite corners to cut four of* Template 25.

***For no-template cutting, cut a 4⅞" square once diagonally from corner to corner to make two of* Template 24.

Sky Blocks

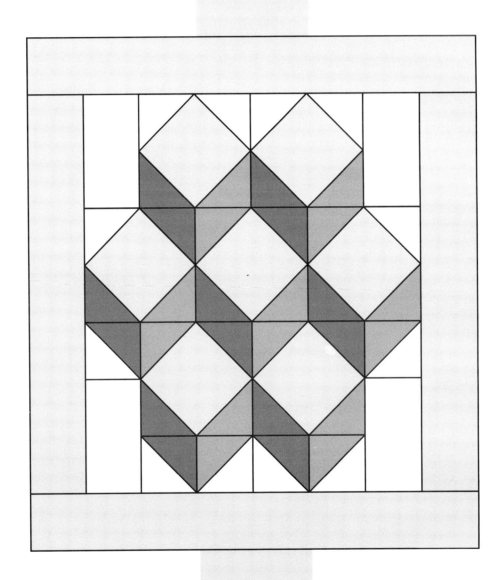

Sky Blocks wall hanging

Block size: 6⅜"
Quilt size: 29" x 32"
Skill level: intermediate

Unit 1

Unit 2

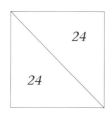
Unit piecing diagram

Materials

(40" fabric)

■ 5" Squares
(light block tops)
7 pieces
7 of *Template 1*

■ 5" Squares (dark shading)
7 pieces
14 of *Template 24**

■ 5" Squares
(medium shading)
7 pieces
14 of *Template 24**

■ Background fabric
⅓ yard
12 of *Template 24**
4 rectangles 3¾" x 6⅞"

■ Borders and binding
1 yard
2 strips 5" x 25½"
   for sides
2 border strips 5" x 31½"
   for top and bottom
binding strips
   (2½" x 3⅞ yards)

■ Lining
1 yard
33" x 36"

■ Batting
33" x 36"

Assembly

1. Because this wall hanging has each unit of shading made from a different fabric (see color picture on page 19), it works best to cut out every piece and lay out the center of the wall hanging completely on a table before beginning to sew.

2. When layout is arranged to your liking, sew blocks together following block drawing and piecing diagram in Baby Blocks (page 45). Make 7 blocks.

3. Join the 2 top row blocks. Sew 2 of the 3¾ x 6⅞ rectangles cut from background fabric to either size of joined blocks. This is row 1.

4. Join the 3 second row blocks together. This is row 2.

5. Join the last 2 blocks together. This is row 3. Sew 3 Unit 1s and 3 Unit 2s. Join 2 Unit 1s and 2 Units 2s, alternating types, to make a unit row. Sew this unit row to the bottom of row 3. Sew 1 Unit 1 and 1 Unit 2 to the tops of 3¾ x 6⅞ rectangles. Following quilt diagram, sew these to either side of row 3 blocks. Join rows.

6. Add side borders to either side of center panel; trim to fit. Add top and bottom borders; trim to fit.

7. Baste together top, batting, and lining. Quilt as desired. Bind to finish.

Needle **Note**

**For no-template cutting, cut diagonally once across a 4⅞" square to make two of Template 24.*

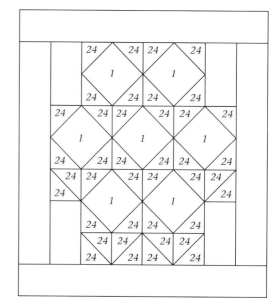
Quilt diagram

Basket

Many versions of the traditional Basket block are available. This is one that can easily be cut from the 5″ squares. When Karen Senet made it, she chose not to use a background fabric for the blocks, so she cut all the pieces except the setting triangles and borders from solid-color 5″ fabric squares. You might wish to use multi-color charm squares to make the baskets in one color and their "fill" in another, or perhaps use dark colors for the baskets and light pastel flowered fabrics for the "fill." Basket blocks can be set on point alternately with plain blocks or separated with sashing as shown.

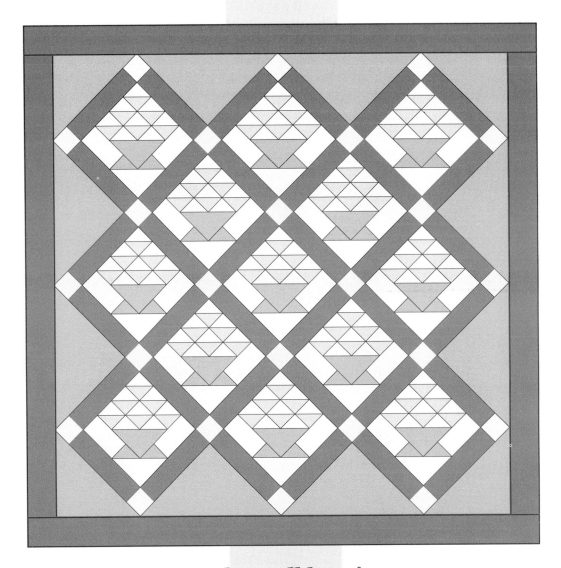

Basket wall hanging

Block size: 8″
Quilt size: 53¼″ x 53¼″
Set 3 x 3 (on point)
Skill level: beginner/intermediate

Materials

(40" fabric)

■ **5" Squares** (basket base)

13 pieces

   13 of *Template 9*

   26 of *Template 4*

■ **5" Squares** (basket "fill")

20 pieces

   78 of *Template 4*

■ **Background fabric**

1 yard

   104 of *Template 4*

   26 of *Template 31*

   13 of *Template 9*

   24 of *Template 2*

     for setting squares

■ **Sashing and setting triangles**

1½ yards

   36 sashing strips

     2½" x 8½"

   4 of *Template 41* for setting

     triangles in corners

   4 squares 12¾" x 12¾"

     (Cut twice diagonally to

     make 8 setting triangles

     for sides.)

■ **Outer border and binding**

1¾ yards

   2 strips 4½" x 47¾"

     for sides

   2 strips 4½" x 55¾"

     for top and bottom

   binding strips

     (2½" x 6⅓ yards)

■ **Lining**

3¼ yards

   2 panels 30" x 57"

■ **Batting**

57" x 57"

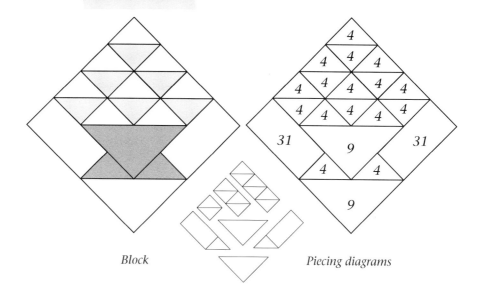

Block   *Piecing diagrams*

Assembly

1. Cut pieces as directed. Referring to the block drawing and piecing diagram, make 13 Basket blocks.

2. Assemble diagonal rows as shown in general directions. Join blocks and sashes alternately to make 5 block rows; join sashes and setting squares alternately to make sash rows. Join 6 sash rows to 5 block rows, alternating types. If setting triangles are too large, trim down to allow ¼" seam allowances, but do not trim until entire quilt top is constructed.

3. Add side borders to either side of center panel; trim to fit. Add top and bottom borders; trim to fit.

4. Baste together top, batting, and lining. Quilt as desired. Bind to finish.

Bear Paw

The Bear Paw is a traditional favorite that is not often made of scrap fabrics. Twelve of these large blocks will make a nap size quilt when set with sashing. Add borders if desired to enlarge the quilt to twin size.

Bear Paw quilt
Block size: 14″
Quilt size: 58″ x 74″
Set 3 x 4
Skill level: intermediate

Materials
(40" fabric)

■ *5" Squares*
(medium fabric)
48 pieces
    48 of *Template 8*

■ *5" Squares* (dark fabric)
56 pieces
    192 of *Template 4*
    32 of *Template 2*

■ *Background*
2⅝ yards
    48 of *Template 43*
    48 of *Template 2*
    192 of *Template 4*
    31 sashing strips
        2½" x 14½"

■ *Borders and binding*
2 yards
    2 strips 4½" x 68½"
        for sides
    2 strips 4½" x 60½"
        for top and bottom
    binding strips
        (2½" x 7⅞ yards)

■ *Lining*
3½ yards
    2 panels 39" x 62"

■ *Batting*
62" x 78"

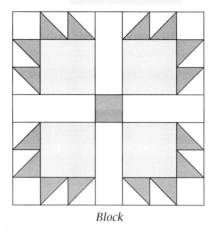

Block

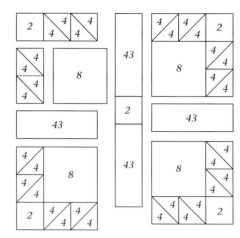

Piecing diagram

Assembly

1. Cut pieces as directed. Sew 1 *Template 4* patch of background fabric and 1 of scrap fabric together to make a square. Combine 4 of these squares with 1 *Template 2* and 1 *Template 8* to make a quarter block. Assemble quarter blocks first, and complete block by joining the quarter blocks with *Templates 2* and *43* as shown in piecing diagram.

2. Join 3 blocks alternately with 4 sashing strips to make a block row. Make 4 block rows.

3. Join 4 setting squares alternately with 3 sashing strips to make a sash row. Make 5 sash rows. Join block rows and sash rows, alternating types. (Add outside borders if desired, but remember that lining and batting will have to be made correspondingly larger.)

4. Baste together top, batting, and lining. Quilt as desired. Bind to finish.

Dresden Daisy

Simple cutting and machine appliqué make this one of the easiest ever versions of the *Dresden Plate* block. The petals are gathered instead of shaped, so it looks more like a puffy flower than a plate. To add to the 1930s look of the pattern, a blanket stitch in black can be used for the appliqué.

Dresden Daisy wall hanging
Block size: 14½"
Quilt size: 35" x 35"
Set 2 x 2
Skill level: intermediate

Materials
(40" fabric)

- **5" Squares** (petals)
32 pieces
   64 of *Template 3*

- **5" Squares** (centers)
4 pieces
   4 of *Template 39*

- **Background fabric**
⅞ yard
   4 squares 15" x 15"

- **Lining for centers**
(muslin or other scrap)
⅛ yard
   4 of *Template 39*

- **Inner border**
¼ yard
   2 strips 1½" x 31½"
      for sides
   2 strips 1½" x 33½"
      for top and bottom

- **Outer border and binding**
⅔ yard
   2 strips 2½" x 33½"
      for sides
   2 strips 2½" x 37½"
      for top and bottom
   binding strips
      (2½" x 4⅓ yards)

- **Lining**
1⅛ yards
   39" x 39"

- **Batting**
39" x 39"

Block

Assembly

1. Cut 32 of the 5" squares in half horizontally to make 64 pieces 2½" x 5" (*Template 3*). Fold these lengthwise with right sides together and sew a ¼" seam across one end. Turn right side out as shown below and press flat with seam in center of back. Make 16 of these "petals" for each daisy (*Fig. 1*).

Cutting line

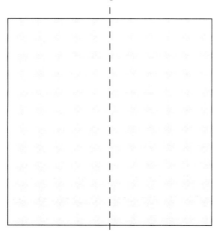

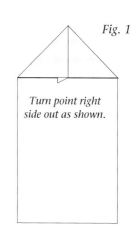

Fold with right sides together and sew ¼" from one end.

Turn point right side out as shown.

Fig. 1

2. Sew 16 petals together using a ¼" seam in the order desired to make a "picket fence" arrangement (*Fig. 2*). Sew the 2 ends together to make a "crown" arrangement.

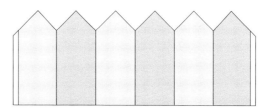

Fig. 2

3. Put heavy thread in the bobbin of your sewing machine and sew with a long stitch around the crown ¼" from the bottom edge.

Gently pull the bobbin thread to gather the petals into a circle with points about 11½" across. Pull top threads to back, and tie securely so that the circle will not slip. Spread out the gathers evenly.

4. Mark the center of your background block. Pat the petals down flat around the outside, and pin into place on the background block. With your ruler, check to see that outside points are equal distances from all 4 sides.

5. If your gathers are too tight, it will not be possible to make the Daisy lay flat. Pin each petal point into place, and check the back of the block to see that the background fabric is still flat. If it is not, loosen the pins and move petal points closer to center.

6. Stitch around the outside of the petals with an open decorative stitch on your sewing machine. (I used the blanket stitch and black thread.) If you prefer, you may hand appliqué the outside rim of the petals.

7. Using *Template 39*, draw a circle with pencil on the wrong sides of 4 of the 5" squares. Do not cut out at this time. Lay each of these pieces on a similar size scrap with the right sides together, matching the straight of grain line. Sew completely around the marked circle. Trim seam allowance to ¼".

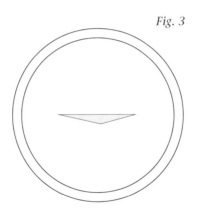

Fig. 3

8. Cut a small slit (about 1½") in the lining (*Fig. 3*). Be careful not to cut the top fabric. Through the slit, turn the piece right side out. Baste around the edge and press to make a smooth circle. It is not necessary to sew up the slit because it will not show.

9. Cut a small scrap of batting about ½" smaller than the circle and lay it on top of the center of the petals. This will cover the gathered seams and puff up the center.

10. Center the circle on the petals and pin securely in place. Check to see that the gathers in the petals are evenly distributed. Machine or hand appliqué the center onto the flower. (If you hand appliqué, remember that you must go all the way through the back of the block with your stitches.)

11. When 4 blocks are completed, sew together. Add inner side borders to either side of center panel; trim to fit. Add outer side borders; trim to fit. Add outer top and bottom borders; trim to fit.

12. Baste together top, batting, and lining. Quilt as desired. Bind to finish.

Dresden Fan

Materials
(40" fabric)

■ **5" Squares** (petals)
26 pieces
   52 of *Template 3*

■ **5" Squares** (centers)
7 pieces or ¼ yard
   13 of *Template 40*

■ **Eyelet lace** (optional)
1½ yards

■ **Background fabric**
1 yard
   13 squares 8" x 8"

   8 triangles for sides–
      Cut two squares
      11½" x 11½"
      diagonally each way from
      corner to corner, so
      straight of grain will be on
      the long outside edge.

   4 triangles for corners –
      Cut two squares
      6¾" x 6¾" diagonally
      once across to make
      corner triangles.

■ **Border and binding**
⅝ yard
   2 strips 2½" x 34½"
      for sides
   2 strips 2½" x 38½"
      for top and bottom
   binding strips
      (2½" x 4½ yards)

■ **Lining**
1¼ yards

■ **Batting**
40" x 40"

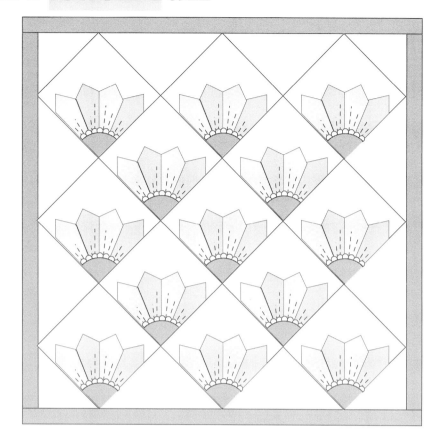

Dresden Fan wall hanging
Block size: 7½"
Quilt size: 36" x 36"
Set 3 x 3 (on point)
Skill level: intermediate

Assembly

1. Sew together 4 of the petals for each block, and use *Template 40* to make the quarter-circle corners. Follow assembly directions for Dresden Daisy. Trim your quarter-circle patches with eyelet lace, if desired, before sewing it over the petals.

2. Appliqué by machine or by hand onto an 8" square of background fabric. Baste outer edges to hold pieces in place during assembly. Remember to add a bit of stuffing behind the quarter circles to hide the covered seam allowances.

3. From background fabric cut setting triangles as directed above.

4. Assemble wall hanging in diagonal rows, adding corner and side triangles as shown in general directions.

5. Baste together top, batting, and lining. Quilt as desired. Bind to finish.

Eccentric Star

Eccentric Star uses a 5" square (*Template 1*) as its centerpiece. All the points are the same shape, but the setting of the pieces gives the star its "eccentricity."

To make a large quilt, set the blocks alternately with plain blocks of the background fabric. Because of their offset points, the blocks are also attractive when set side by side.

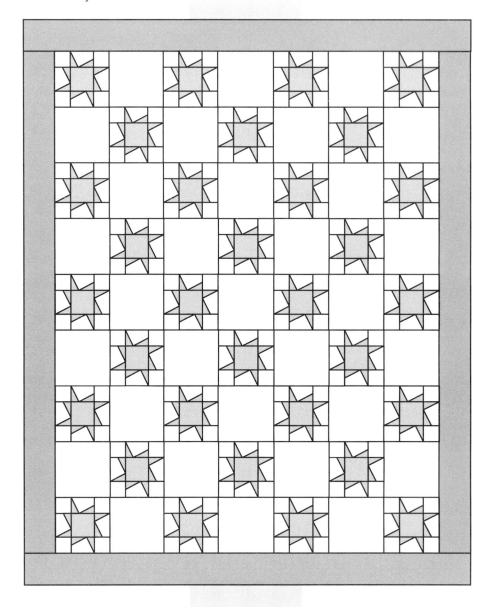

Eccentric Star quilt
Block size: 10½"
Quilt size: 79½" x 100½"
Set 7 x 9
Skill level: beginner/intermediate

Materials

(40" fabric)

■ 5" Squares
96 pieces
  32 of *Template 1*
  128 of *Template 15*

■ Background fabric
6¼ yards
  128 of *Template 21*
  128 of *Template 18*
  31 squares 11" x 11"

■ Border and binding
2⅞ yards
  2 strips 3½" x 97"
    for sides
  2 strips 3½" x 82"
    for top and bottom
  binding strips
    (2½" x 10½ yards)

■ Lining
7⅛ yards
  3 panels 36" x 84"

■ Batting
84" x 105"

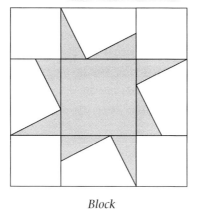

Block

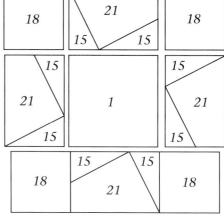

Piecing diagram

Unit 1

Assembly

1. Cut alternate plain squares from background fabric before cutting other pieces.

2. Make 4 Unit 1s. Referring to block drawing and piecing diagrams, sew 2 *Template 18* patches to either side of 2 Unit 1s to make 2 rows. Sew 2 Unit 1s to either side of *Template 1* patch (5" square) to make 1 row. Sew rows together, alternating types, to make block. Make 32 blocks.

3. Referring to quilt diagram, join 4 pieced blocks and 3 plain blocks, alternating types, to form row. Make 5 rows of this type. Referring to quilt diagram, join 4 plain blocks and 3 pieced blocks, alternating types, to form row. Make 4 rows of this type. Sew rows together, alternating types.

4. Add side borders to either side of center panel; trim to fit. Add top and bottom borders; trim to fit.

5. Baste together top, batting, and lining. Quilt as desired. Bind to finish.

Needle **Note**

Two 5" squares will make all eight star points! Select two 5" squares to blend with each center for the star points.

Evening Star

Evening Star is a fine old pattern than lends itself to many variations. As a scrap quilt, this is attractive when you make every star point from a different print in the same color family.

Any combination of these blocks will make an attractive full-size quilt as well. When set side by side, this pattern tends to loose its distinctiveness so that adding sashing between the blocks is your best bet.

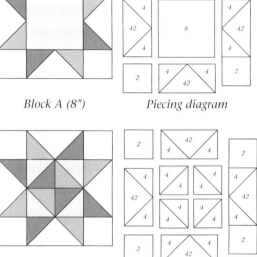

Block A (8") — Piecing diagram

Block B (8") — Piecing diagram

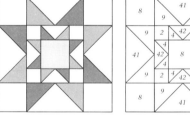

Block C (16") — Piecing diagram

Double Evening Star wall hanging

Block size: 8" and 16"

Quilt size: 36" x 36"

Set 3 x 3

Skill level: beginner/intermediate

Materials

(40″ fabric)

■ **5″ Squares** (stars)
35 pieces
  5 of *Template 8*
  8 of *Template 9*
  104 of *Template 4*

■ **Background fabric**
⅞ yard
  4 of *Template 8*
  4 of *Template 41*
  36 of *Template 2*
  36 of *Template 42*

■ **Border, sashing strips,
and binding**
⅞ yard
  8 pieces 4½″ x 8½″
    for sashing
  2 strips 2½″ x 34½″
    for sides
  2 strips 2½″ x 38½″
    for top and bottom
  binding strips
    (2½″ x 4½ yards)

■ **Lining**
1¼ yards

■ **Batting**
40″ x 40″

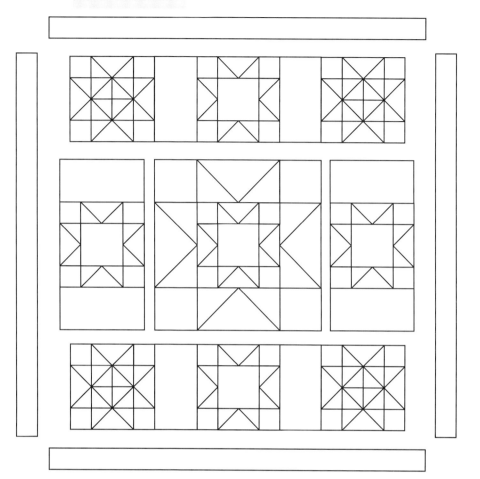

Quilt assembly diagram

Assembly

1. Cut border pieces first. Cut other patches as described.

2. Following piecing diagrams, make 4 Block As, 4 Block Bs, and 1 Block C.

3. Referring to quilt assembly diagram, join together 2 Block Bs, 1 Block A, and 2 sashing strips (4½ x 8½), alternating types. Make 2 rows of this kind.

4. Sew a sashing strip to top and bottom of your remaining 2 Block As. Join these units to either side of Block C, following quilt assembly diagram. Sew the 3 rows together, alternating types.

5. Add side borders to either side of center panel; trim to fit. Add top and bottom borders; trim to fit.

6. Baste together top, batting, and lining. Quilt as desired. Bind to finish.

Evening in America

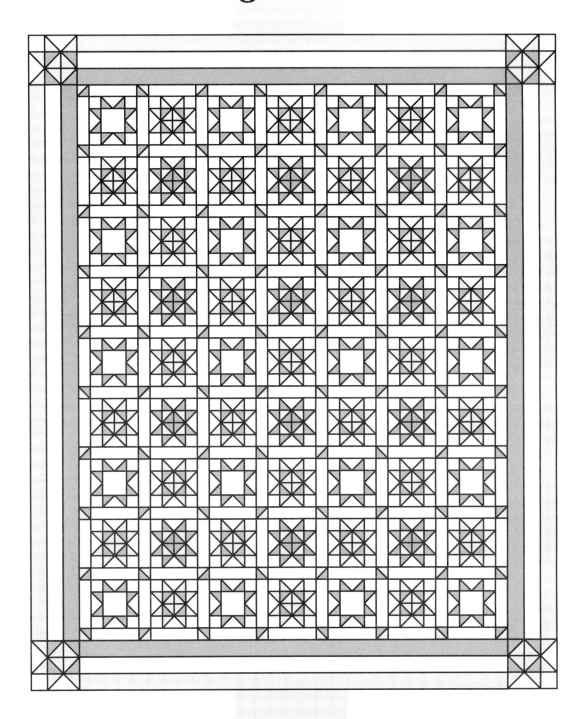

Evening in America quilt
Block size: 8"
Quilt size: 84" x 104"
Set 7 x 9
Skill level: intermediate

Materials

(40" fabric)

■ **5" Squares** (red)
133 pieces
   532 of *Template 4*

■ **5" Squares** (blue)
131 pieces
   524 of *Template 4*

■ **Background and white borders**
9¾ yards
   256 of *Template 2*
   20 of *Template 8*
   260 of *Template 42*
   142 sashing strips
      2½" x 8½"
   2 strips 2½" x 74½"
   2 strips 2½" x 94½"

■ **Blue inner borders**
2⅞ yards
   2 strips 2½" x 74½"
   2 strips 2½" x 94½"

■ **Red outer borders and binding**
2⅞ yards
   2 strips 2½" x 74½"
   2 strips 2½" x 94½"
   binding strips
      (2½" x 11 yards)

■ **Lining**
7⅝ yards
   3 panels 36" x 88"

■ **Batting**
88" x 108"

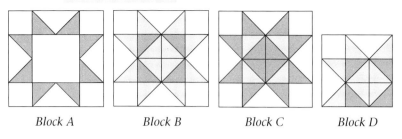

Block A   Block B   Block C   Block D

Block E   Block E piecing diagrams

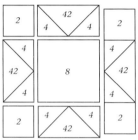
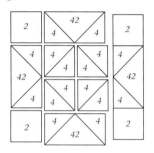
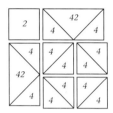

Block A piecing diagram   Block B & C piecing diagram   Block D piecing diagram

Assembly

1. Assemble blocks as shown in piecing diagrams, making 20 Block As, 31 Block Bs, 12 Block Cs, 4 Block Ds, and 80 Block Es. Blue is indicated by darker color, red by medium color. Block D is the corner block in the border. Block E is the setting square.

2. Assemble quilt blocks in horizontal rows, alternating types according to the quilt drawing, and separating blocks by sashing strips. Make 9 block rows.

3. Join together setting blocks (Block E), alternating direction according to the quilt drawing, and sashing strips alternately to make sash row. Make 10 sash rows.

4. Make side borders by sewing together 1 red, 1 white, and 1 blue border strip (2½" x 94½"). Make 2 borders of this type. Make top and bottom borders by sewing together 1 red, 1 white, and 1 blue border strip (2½" x 74¼"). Make 2 borders of this type.

5. Sew side borders to center panel; trim to fit. Measure top and bottom of quilt top and cut the top and bottom borders to fit. Add Blocks D to either end of each border, following direction in quilt diagram. Finish assembling quilt by adding top and bottom borders.

6. Baste together top, batting, and lining. Quilt as desired. Bind to finish.

Gentleman's Fancy

Gentleman's Fancy, a traditional block, uses only one size piece that's cut without using a template from a 5″ square. Just make two diagonal cuts from corner to corner. (See instructions for *Template 5* on page 137.)

You can use 100 of your 5″ squares in dark print fabrics and a background fabric for the light squares to make 16 blocks. This also can be a very attractive multi-colored scrap quilt. Mix your own scrap pieces (cut from *Template 5*) freely in the design to achieve the mixture of darks and lights that you desire.

The addition of alternate blocks of plain fabric and multiple borders will make it possible to create a 72″ x 92″ quilt.

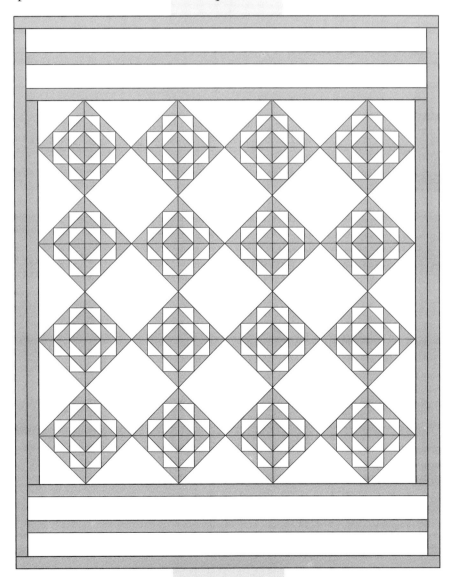

Gentleman's Fancy quilt
Block size: 11¼″
Quilt size: 72″ x 92″
Set 4 x 4 (on point)
Skill level: intermediate

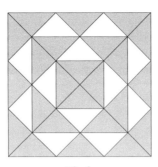

Block *Piecing diagram*

Materials

(40" fabric)

■ 5" Squares
96 pieces

384 of *Template 5*

■ Background fabric
4⅛ yards

192 of *Template 5*

4 strips 4½" x 70½"

9 squares 11¾" x 11¾"
for alternate plain blocks

3 squares 17¾" x 17¾"
(Cut twice diagonally to
make 12 setting triangles
for the sides.)

2 squares 9" x 9"
(Cut once diagonally to
make corner triangles.)

■ Borders and binding
2⅔ yards

2 strips 2½" x 66½"
for inner sides

4 strips 2½" x 70½"
for horizontal borders

2 strips 2½" x 74½"
for top and bottom
borders

2 strips 2½" x 90½"
for side borders

binding strips
(2½" x 9⅝ yards)

■ Lining
5⅛ yards

2 panels 39" x 96"

■ Batting
76" x 96"

Assembly

1. Cut borders first and set aside. Cut alternate plain squares, setting triangles, and sashing strips and set aside.

2. Cut the triangles for your blocks using *Template 5* or the no-template method of cutting from 5" squares (see page 137).

3. Referring to block drawing and piecing diagram, assemble 16 blocks. Join pieced blocks, plain squares, and setting and corner triangles into diagonal rows as shown in the general directions for quilts set on point. Make 7 rows.

4. Sew 2 light and 2 dark border strips (70½" long) alternately as shown in *Fig. 1* below to make multiple border strips.

Fig. 1

5. Add side borders (66½") to either side of center panel; trim to fit. Add top and bottom multiple border strips; trim to fit. Add outer side borders (90½"); trim to fit. Add outer top and bottom borders (74½"); trim to fit.

6. Baste together top, batting, and lining. Quilt as desired. Bind to finish.

Needle **Note**

If all the triangles are made from a 100-piece 5" square die-cut fabric packet, 11 blocks can be made. In this case, sort the lights and darks carefully to preserve the design.

Mayflower

Mayflower uses a clever piecing system to make this intricate-looking block easy to create. All the *Template 5* pieces are cut with a fast, no-template method from 5″ squares to make it even easier.

Even though it is fairly simple to piece, Mayflower is a large, complex-appearing block, and it will be best to set the blocks apart with sashing as shown in the quilt drawing.

Mayflower quilt
Block size: 15″
Quilt size: 78″ x 95″
Set 4 x 5
Skill level: intermediate

Materials

(40" fabric)

■ 5" Squares
100 pieces

400 of *Template 5*
for flower petals

■ Background fabric
4⅝ yards

640 of *Template 27*
80 of *Template 29*
80 of *Template 30*
49 strips 2½" x 15½"
for sashing

■ Squares for flower centers
⅜ yard

80 of *Template 28*

■ Accent color for block center and setting squares
½ yard

80 of *Template 27*
30 of *Template 2* for setting squares

■ Border and binding
2⅝ yards

2 side borders
4½" x 89½" for sides
2 end borders
4½" x 80½" for top and bottom
binding strips
(2½" x 10⅛ yards)

■ Lining
6⅞ yards

3 panels 34" x 82"

■ Batting
82" x 99"

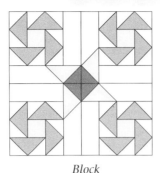

Block

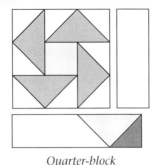

Quarter-block

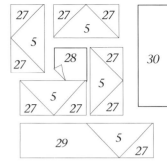

Quarter-block piecing diagram

Unit 1

Unit 2

Unit 3

Unit 4

Assembly

1. Cut pieces as directed.

2. Sew block together in quarter-block sections. Make Unit 1 from 1 *Template 5* patch and 2 *Template 27* patches. Referring to piecing diagram, join 4 Unit 1s to *Template 28* patch to make Unit 2. First sew the half seam; then continue adding Unit 1s counter-clockwise around the center until the last seam finishes the open half seam left in the beginning.

3. Sew Unit 3 (*Template 30*) to right side of Unit 2. Join Unit 4 to the bottom. Sew 4 of these quarter blocks together, rotating each quarter block as shown in the block drawing, to make the block. Make 20 blocks.

4. Add sashes that fall between blocks and alternately join blocks and sashes to complete block rows. Make 5 block rows.

5. Join 5 setting squares and 4 sashes alternately to complete sash rows. Make 6 sash rows. Join block rows and sash rows, alternating types, to assemble the quilt top.

6. Add side borders to either side of center panel; trim to fit. Add top and bottom borders; trim to fit.

7. Baste together top, batting, and lining. Quilt as desired. Bind to finish.

Mosaic I

Two versions of the Mosaic block are given. Because they are nearly identical (except for color placement), I have chosen to combine their directions.

All the pieces are cut from the same template. Each block contains 16 units consisting of a light triangle and a dark triangle sewn together. The difference in Block A and Block B results from the arrangement of these units.

There is a choice of block size given. The larger size, using *Template 6*, is the easiest to cut and the most economical use of your 5″ squares, but the piece sizes may be larger than you are used to working with.

A wall hanging arrangement is given using the smaller size (*Template 4*), and a twin-size quilt is shown using the blocks in the larger size. Both tops are assembled by alternating Blocks A and B.

Mosaic I wall hanging
Block size: 8″
Quilt size: 30″ x 30″
Set 3 x 3
Skill level: beginner/intermediate

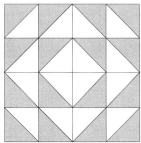
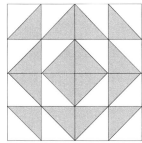
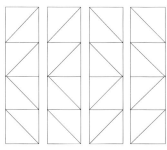

*Block A–darker colors
on outside*
  *Block B–lighter colors
on outside*
  Piecing diagram

Materials

(40" fabric)

■ **5" Squares** (dark triangles)
36 pieces
144 of *Template 4*

■ **5" Squares** (light triangles)
36 pieces
144 of *Template 4*

■ **Inner border**
¼ yard
2 strips 1½" x 26½"
for sides
2 strips 1½" x 28½"
for top and bottom

■ **Outer border and binding**
⅝ yard
2 strips 2½" x 28½"
for sides
2 strips 2½" x 32½"
for top and bottom
binding strips
(2½" x 3⅞ yards)

■ **Lining**
1 yard
1 panel 34" x 34"

■ **Batting**
34" x 34"

Assembly

1. Cut triangles using *Template 4*.

2. Assemble small square Unit 1s by sewing 1 light triangle to 1 dark triangle. Each block requires 16 Unit 1s.

3. Referring to block drawings and piecing diagram, arrange units into blocks. Make 5 Block As and 4 Block Bs.

4. Sew 2 Block As and 1 Block B together, alternating types, to make top row. Repeat to make bottom row. Sew 2 Block Bs and 1 block A together, alternating types, to make middle row. Sew the 3 rows together.

5. Add side inner borders to either side of center panel; trim to fit. Add top and bottom inner borders; trim to fit. Add outer side borders; trim to fit. Add outer top and bottom borders; trim to fit.

6. Baste together top, batting, and lining. Quilt as desired. Bind to finish.

Unit 1

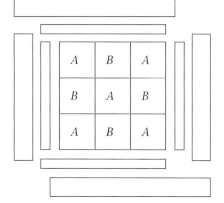

Quilt assembly diagram

Needle **Note**

The quilt project has background fabric yardage given for the lighter triangles, but if you can get a really good color contrast using your scraps, this quilt is spectacular when it is made from light and dark scraps.

Mosaic I

Mosaic I quilt
Block size: 16½"
Quilt size: 61½" x 94½"
Set 3 x 5
Skill level: beginner/intermediate

Materials

(40" fabric)

■ *5" Squares*
120 pieces
240 of *Template 6*

■ *Background triangles and inner borders*
2½ yards
240 of *Template 6*
2 strips 2½" x 84½"
   for sides
2 strips 2½" x 55½"
   for top and bottom

■ *Outer borders and binding*
2⅝ yards
2 strips 4½" x 88½"
   for sides
2 strips 4½" x 63½"
   for top and bottom
binding strips
   (2½" x 9¼ yards)

■ *Lining*
5½ yards
2 panels 34" x 99"

■ *Batting*
66" x 99"

Assembly

1. Cut colored triangles from medium and dark 5" print squares, using *Template 6* (or simply cut once diagonally across the 5" square).

2. Cut border strips from background fabric first. Cut background triangles as directed.

3. Assemble square units by sewing one colored triangle to one background triangle. Each block requires 16 of these units.

4. Make 8 Block As and 7 Block Bs, following the directions given in Mosaic I wall hanging. Referring to the quilt diagram, sew 3 blocks together in horizontal rows, alternating A and B blocks, following the directions in the wall hanging. Make 5 rows. Sew rows together.

5. Add side inner borders to either side of center panel; trim to fit. Add top and bottom inner borders; trim to fit. Add outer side borders; trim to fit. Add outer top and bottom borders; trim to fit.

6. Baste together top, batting, and lining. Quilt as desired. Bind to finish.

Needle **Note**

Here's a good technique to speed up finishing your quilt: Take running stitches along the very edge of the quilt "sandwich" before sewing on the binding. The stitching holds all the layers together so the binding goes on easily– with no time wasted trying to adjust the layers.

Mosaic II

Mosaic II gives a boxy or dimensional effect that makes it appear to be set on the diagonal. Its component pieces and assembly directions are identical to those for Mosaic I. Just be very careful to follow the shaded diagrams to see how the units are arranged. Note that only the position of the four inner units is changed.

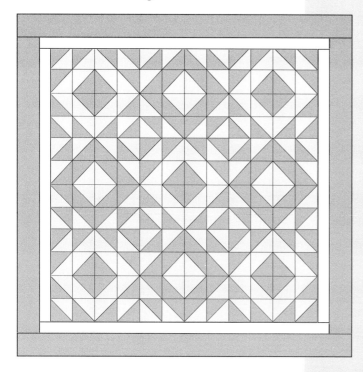

Mosaic II wall hanging
Block size: 8″
Quilt size: 30″ x 30″
Set 3 x 3
Skill level: beginner/intermediate

Mosaic II quilt
Block size: 16½″
Quilt size: 61½″ x 94½″
Set 3 x 5
Skill level: beginner/intermediate

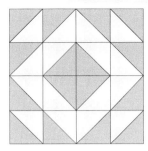

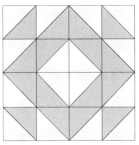

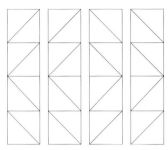

Block A – darker colors on outside   *Block B – lighter colors on outside*   *Piecing diagram*

Wall Hanging Materials

(40" fabric)

■ All fabric requirements are the same as for Mosaic I wall hanging.

Wall Hanging Assembly

All directions are the same as for Mosaic I wall hanging, except that the orientation of the inner units within the blocks is different. Consult shaded drawings to make sure that blocks are correct before assembling.

Quilt Materials

(40" fabric)

■ All fabric requirements are the same as for Mosaic I quilt.

Quilt Assembly

All directions are the same as for Mosaic I quilt, except that the orientation of the inner units within the blocks is different. Consult shaded drawings to make sure that blocks are correct before assembling.

Northern Lights

Northern Lights has a strong diagonal appearance and is shown arranged in a setting that radiates from the center of the quilt. Choose a good contrast between the colors for the design and the background fabric. Use your lightest 5″ squares for two of the center squares as shown in the block drawing.

Northern Lights quilt
Block size: 8″
Quilt size: 72″ x 88″
Set 8 x 10
Skill level: beginner

Materials
(40" fabric)

■ 5" Squares
200 pieces
480 of *Template 2*
320 of *Template 4*

■ Background fabric
3 yards
320 of *Template 2*
160 of *Template 9*

■ Borders and binding
2½ yards
2 strips 4½" x 82½"
  for sides
2 strips 4½" x 74½"
  for top and bottom
binding strips
  (2½" x 9⅓ yards)

■ Lining
5⅛ yards
2 panels
39" x 92"

■ Batting
76" x 92"

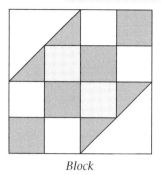

Block

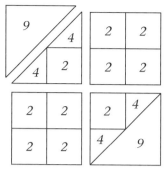

Piecing diagram

Assembly

1. Sort out 40 of your lightest colored squares to cut 160 *Template 2* pieces. Referring to block drawing and piecing diagram, make 80 blocks.

2. Arrange blocks in 10 rows of 8 blocks each in a setting that radiates out from the quilt's center. To do this, reverse the direction of the first 4 blocks in the first 5 rows and the last 4 blocks in the last 5 rows.

3. Add side borders to either side of the center panel; trim to fit. Add top and bottom borders, trim to fit.

4. Baste together top, batting, and lining. Quilt as desired. Bind to finish.

Southwestern Lights Assembly

Northern Lights can be used alone in the quilt described above, or it can be combined with Anvil block to make an interesting quilt with a Southwestern flavor.

Construct this quilt by making 18 Anvil blocks and 18 Northern Lights blocks. Cut 24 corner triangles from 12 6⅝" squares. Cut each across once diagonally. Cut 60 setting triangles from 15 12⅝" squares. Cut each across diagonally.

If you make the horizontal bands 3" wide, the quilt will measure 67½" x 94½". This would make an interesting design project for the intermediate quilter. Follow the quilt diagram shown here and the directions given for piecing the Northern Lights and Anvil blocks to make the quilt.

Ohio Star

Directions are given for two colorations of Ohio Star. *Template 5* is one of the easiest to cut–simply two diagonal cuts across a 5″ square. It works with many settings, but tends to lose the distinctiveness of design if the blocks are set side by side. The quilt shown uses alternate plain blocks to show off your quilting.

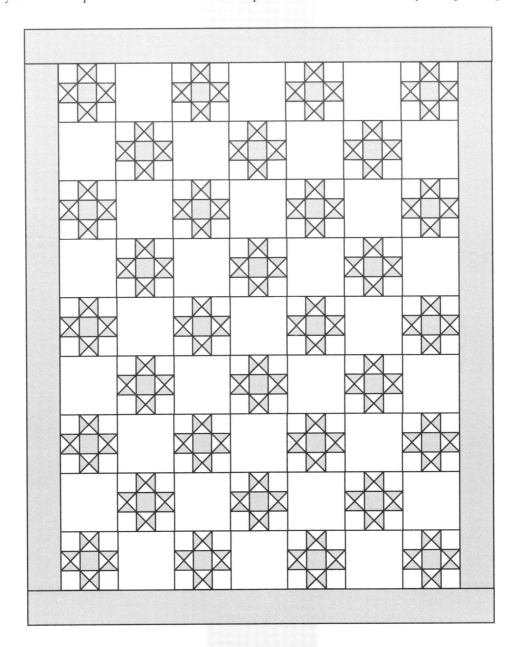

Ohio Star quilt
Block size: 11¼″
Quilt size: 86¾″ x 109¼″
Set 7 x 9
Skill level: beginner/intermediate

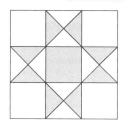
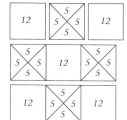
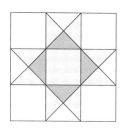

Block   Piecing diagram   Color variation block

Materials

(40" fabric)

■ 5" Squares
96 pieces
 32 of *Template 12*
 256 of *Template 5*
■ Background fabric
7⅛ yards
 31 squares 11¾" x 11¾"
 256 of *Template 5*
 128 of *Template 12*
■ Borders and binding
3⅛ yards
 2 strips 4½" x 103½"
  for sides
 2 strips 4½" x 89½"
  for top and bottom
 binding strips
  (2½" x 11⅛ yards)
■ Lining
7⅝ yards
 3 panels 39" x 91"
■ Batting
91" x 113"

Materials for the same quilt with the color variation block shown above will be:

■ 5" Squares
(light star pieces)
96 pieces
 32 of *Template 12*
 256 of *Template 5*
■ 5" Squares
(dark inner star)
32 pieces
 128 of *Template 5*
■ Background fabric
6⅝ yards
 31 squares 11¾" x 11¾"
 128 of *Template 5*
 128 of *Template 12*
■ Borders, binding, lining, and batting are same as above.

Assembly

1. Referring to block diagrams and piecing diagrams, make 32 blocks, in the color variation of your choice.

2. Join 4 Ohio Star blocks with 3 plain blocks, alternating types, to make block row. Make 5 block rows of this type.

3. Join 4 plain blocks with 3 Ohio Star blocks, alternating types, to make block row. Make 4 block rows of this type. Join rows together, alternating types according to the quilt diagram.

4. Add side borders to either side of center panel; trim to fit. Add top and bottom borders; trim to fit.

5. Baste together top, batting, and lining. Quilt as desired. Bind to finish.

Old Maid's Puzzle

For a really intricate looking wall hanging, combine 5″ squares of white prints with 5″ squares of a darker color to make this Old Maid's Puzzle block. If you prefer, the lighter pieces could all be made from one background fabric.

This same block can be made with *Template 6* (substituting for *Template 4*) and *Template 7* (substituting for *Template 2*), which will give you a 16½″ x 16½″ unit. You will need to sew four of these units together to create the 33″ block. Separate large blocks with sashing strips to keep the top better organized. (Directions for making a large quilt in this manner are given.)

Old Maid's Puzzle wall hanging
Block size: 8″
Quilt size: 38″ x 38″
Set 4 x 4
Skill level: beginner/intermediate

Materials
(40" fabric)

■ **5" Squares** (dark)
54 pieces
  56 of *Template 2*
  160 of *Template 4*

■ **5" Squares** (light)
50 pieces
  40 of *Template 2*
  160 of *Template 4*

■ **Light inside border**
¼ yard
  2 strips 1½" x 34½"
    for sides
  2 strips 1½" x 36½"
    for top and bottom

■ **Dark outside border and binding**
⅝ yard
  2 strips 2½" x 36½"
    for sides
  2 strips 2½" x 40"
    for top and bottom
  binding strips
    (2½" x 4⅜ yards)

■ **Lining**
1¼ yards
  40" x 40"

■ **Batting**
42" x 42"

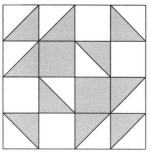

Block A

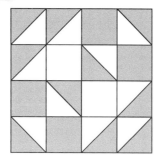

Block B

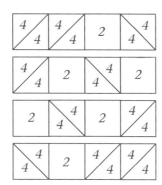

Piecing diagram

Assembly

1. Make 4 Block As and 12 Block Bs following block drawings and piecing diagram.

2. Referring to quilt drawing, sew 4 Block Bs together to make block row, noting carefully the direction that each block is turned. Make 2 rows of this type. These will be the top and bottom rows. Next, sew 1 Block B, 2 Block As, and 1 Block B, in that order, to make second block row, noting carefully the direction that each block is turned. Make 2 rows of this type. These will be the middle 2 rows. Sew all 4 rows together.

3. Add inner side borders to either side of center panel; trim to fit. Add inner top and bottom borders; trim to fit. Add outer side borders; trim to fit. Add top and bottom borders; trim to fit.

4. Baste together top, batting, and lining. Quilt as desired. Bind to finish.

Old Maid's Puzzle

Old Maid's Puzzle quilt
Block size: 33″
Quilt size: 111″ x 111″
Set 3 x 3
Skill level: intermediate

Materials

(40" fabric)

■ 5" Squares
268 pieces

   360 of *Template 6*

   72 of *Template 7*

   16 of *Template 18*
     for setting squares

■ Background, sashing, and binding
9 yards

   360 of *Template 6*

   144 of *Template 7*

   21 sashing strips
     3½" x 33½"

   binding strips
     (2½" x 12⅞ yards)

■ Lining
9⅝ yards

   3 panels 39" x 115"

■ Batting
115" x 115"

Assembly

1. Make 36 quarter-block units using Old Maid's Puzzle Block A as your guide. Arrange these in groups of 4, turning each as shown in the quilt drawing, to make the large quilt block. Make 9 large blocks.

2. Join 4 sashing strips alternately with 3 blocks to make block row. Make 3 block rows.

3. Join 4 setting squares alternately with 3 sashing strips to make sash row. Make 4 sash rows. Join block rows and sash rows, alternating types.

4. Baste together top, batting, and lining. Quilt as desired. Bind to finish.

Needle **Note**

If your fabric-finding technique needs speeding up to reduce the time spent searching for fabrics on hand, try this: Organize stored fabric by color in clear plastic boxes. Large plastic sandwich boxes make an ideal place to store your precut 5" squares!

Open Box

A minimum of special cutting is used in Open Box. Only the background triangles are cut using templates. This block can be set side by side, or you can separate blocks with sashing strips.

Open Box quilt
Block size: 12¾"
Quilt size: 69" x 83¾"
Set 4 x 5
Skill level: beginner

Materials
(40" fabric)

■ *5" Squares*
100 pieces

■ *Background fabric*
3¼ yards
80 of *Template 24*
80 of *Template 25*
25 sashing strips
2½" x 13¼"
6 sashing strips
2½" x 63½"

■ *Borders and binding*
2⅓ yards
2 strips 4½" x 77¾"
for sides
2 strips 4½" x 71½"
for top and bottom
binding strips
(2½" x 9 yards)

■ *Lining*
6⅛ yards
3 panels 30" x 73"

■ *Batting*
73" x 88"

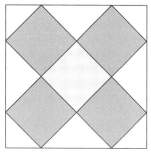

Block

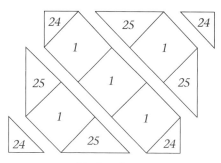

Piecing diagram

Assembly

1. Sort out 20 of your lightest squares to use for the centers of the blocks. Sort the remaining 80 squares into groups of 4 of approximately equal color value. Use 1 light square and 1 group of 4 for each block.

2. Referring to block drawing and piecing diagram, make 20 blocks.

3. Join together 5 short sashing strips and 4 blocks, alternating types, to make a block row. Make 5 block rows.

4. Referring to quilt drawing, join block rows and long sashing strips, alternating types.

5. Add side borders to either side of center panel; trim to fit. Add top and bottom borders; trim to fit.

6. Baste together top, batting, and lining. Quilt as desired. Bind to finish.

Needle **Note**

Before joining rows with long sashes, accurately measure and use pins to mark positions for blocks and sashes. Short sashes should visually connect; accurate measuring and sewing will give you perfect results.

Scrap Star

Scrap Star is a versatile design that can use scraps of all colors in a splendid medley, or it can be closely color coordinated if you prefer.

Scrap Star block is offered here in two different sizes. The 16" block is shown in a wall hanging, and the 24" block is featured in a quilt. The larger size block offers some fairly large expanses of plain fabric to show off your best quilting.

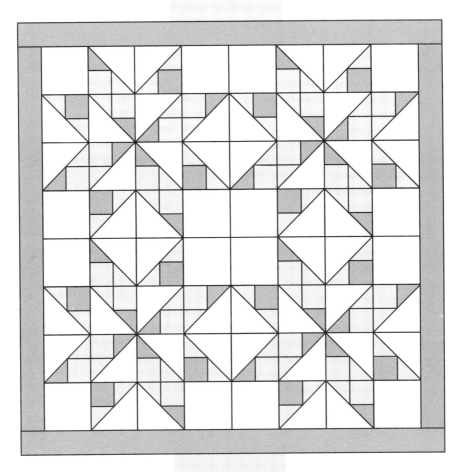

Scrap Star wall hanging
Block size: 16"
Quilt size: 40" x 40"
Set 2 x 2
Skill level: beginner/intermediate

Materials

(40" fabric)

■ 5" Squares
36 pieces
   48 of *Template 2*
   96 of *Template 4*

■ Background fabric
¾ yard
   16 of *Template 8*
   48 of *Template 9*

■ Borders and binding
1¼ yards
   2 strips 4½" x 34½"
      for sides
   2 strips 4½" x 42½"
      for top and bottom
   binding strips
      (2½" x 5 yards)

■ Lining
2½ yards
   2 panels 23" x 44"

■ Batting
44" x 44"

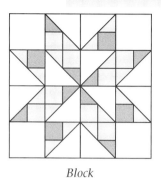

Block

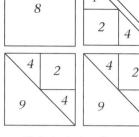

Unit 1 piecing diagram–
make 4 for each 16" block

Assembly

1. Cut pieces as directed. Note that the Unit 1 piecing diagram is given for one-fourth of the block. Make 4 of these for each of 4 blocks, 16 units in all. Combine into 4 blocks, carefully noting the direction that each unit is turned, and assemble into quilt top.

2. Add side borders to either side of center panel; trim to fit. Add top and bottom borders; trim to fit.

3. Baste together top, batting, and lining. Quilt as desired. Bind to finish.

Needle **Note**

After you've finished piecing all the blocks (for this quilt or any quilt), double-check the measurements of each one. Any larger or smaller than they're supposed to be? If so, plan to compensate for minor differences by adjusting seam allowances when you add the borders. If the differences are sizable, however, you should take the too-large or too-small blocks apart and re-piece them. Better to make adjustments now than to struggle with mismatched blocks, borders, and sashes later.

Scrap Star

Scrap Star quilt
Block size: 24″
Quilt size: 92″ x 119″
Set 3 x 4
Skill level: beginner/intermediate

Materials

(40" fabric)

■ 5" Squares
236 pieces

432 of *Template 2*

432 of *Template 4*

20 of *Template 18* for setting squares

■ Background fabric
6¾ yards

48 of *Template 19*

144 of *Template 20*

31 sashing strips 3½" x 24½"

■ Borders and binding
3⅓ yards

2 strips 4½" x 113½" for sides

2 strips 4½" x 94½" for top and bottom

binding strips (2½" x 12¼ yards)

■ Lining
10¼ yards

3 panels 33" x 123"

■ Batting
96" x 123"

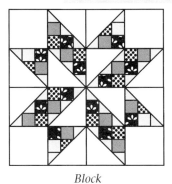

Block

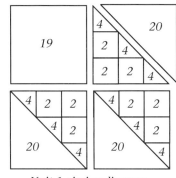

*Unit 1 piecing diagram—
make 4 for each 24" block*

Assembly

1. Referring to block drawing and unit piecing diagram, sew 4 Unit 1s together, carefully noting the direction that each unit is turned, to make 1 block. Make 12 blocks.

2. Join 4 sashing strips and 3 blocks, alternating types, to make block rows. Make 4 block rows.

3. Join 4 setting squares and 3 sashing strips to make sash rows. Make 5 sash rows. Join block rows and sash rows, alternately to assemble the quilt top.

4. Add side borders to either side of center panel trim to fit. Add top and bottom borders; trim to fit.

5. Baste together top, batting, and lining. Quilt as desired. Bind to finish.

Simple Diamond

Simple Diamond couldn't be simpler! Each piece uses *Template 6*, which is easily cut from a 5″ square with a single diagonal cut from corner to corner. Color sorting of your charm squares will enable you to give this block its distinctive appearance. This design would also be particularly adaptable to using two different color families of 5″ squares.

Three quilt versions are included with arrangements of this simple block. You may wish to use a background fabric for the darkest (or lightest) pieces. As with almost all the quilts in this book, the finished quilt size is easily adjustable by adding or subtracting blocks.

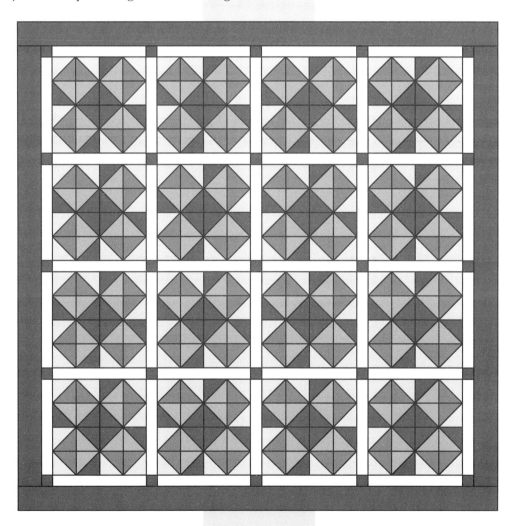

Diamond in a Whirl quilt

Block size: 16½″
Quilt size: 84″ x 84″
Set 4 x 4
Skill level: beginner

Materials

(40" fabric)

■ 5" Squares
256 pieces
light–128 of *Template 6*

medium light–128 of *Template 6*

medium dark–128 of *Template 6*

dark–128 of *Template 6*

■ Setting squares
¼ yard
25 of *Template 2*

■ Sashing strips
1½ yards
40 strips 2½" x 17"

■ Border and binding
2⅝ yards
2 strips 4½" x 78½" for sides

2 strips 4½" x 86½" for top and bottom

binding strips (2½" x 9⅞ yards)

■ Lining
7⅓ yards
3 panels 30" x 88"

■ Batting
88" x 88"

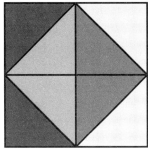

Block

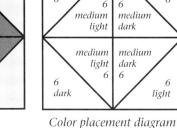

Color placement diagram

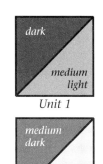

Unit 1

Unit 2

Assembly

1. Sort your 5" squares into 4 groups: light, medium light, medium dark, and dark. Cut each square diagonally to create the piece designated *Template 6*.

2. Sew dark triangles to medium light triangles to make Unit 1s; sew medium dark triangles to light triangles to make Unit 2s. Each block contains 2 each of these units. Assemble units as shown in color-placement diagram to make block.

3. Arrange blocks into groups of 4, rotating around the center to make Unit 3. Make 16 Unit 3s.

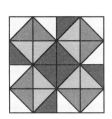

Unit 3

4. Alternately join 4 Unit 3s and 5 sashing strips to complete unit row. Make 4 unit rows.

5. Join 5 setting squares and 4 sashing strips, alternating types, to complete sash row. Make 5 sash rows. Join unit rows and sash rows alternately to assemble quilt top.

6. Add side borders to either side of center panel; trim to fit. Add top and bottom borders; trim to fit.

7. Baste together top, batting, and lining. Quilt as desired. Bind to finish.

Harlequin Diamonds

Materials
(40" fabric)

■ *5" Squares*
352 pieces
light–176 of *Template 6*
medium light–176 of *Template 6*
medium dark–176 of *Template 6*
dark–176 of *Template 6*

■ *Sashing strips, borders, and binding*
2¾ yards
5 strips 2½" x 93¼" for sashing strips and side borders
2 strips 4½" x 78½" for top and bottom borders
binding strips (2½" x 10¼ yards)

■ *Lining*
6¾ yards
3 panels 35" x 80"

■ *Batting*
80" x 103"

Harlequin Diamonds quilt
Block size: 8¼"
Quilt size: 76" x 98¾"
Set 8 x 11
Skill level: beginner

Assembly

1. Follow direction Nos. 1-2 in Diamond in a Whirl to make 88 blocks.

2. Assemble 4 vertical rows of blocks as shown in the quilt drawing, 2 blocks wide and 11 blocks down, carefully noting the direction each block is turned. Join these vertical rows together with sashing strips.

3. Add side borders to either side of center panel; trim to fit. Add top and bottom borders; trim to fit.

4. Baste together top, batting, and lining. Quilt as desired. Bind to finish.

Diamond Shadows

Materials
(40" fabric)

■ 5" Squares
352 pieces
light–176 of *Template 6*
medium light–176 of
Template 6
medium dark–176 of
Template 6
dark–176 of *Template 6*

■ Borders and binding
2¾ yards
2 strips 4½" x 93½"
for side borders
2 strips 4½" x 76½"
for top and bottom
borders
binding strips
(2½" x 10⅛ yards)

■ Lining
5¾ yards
2 panels 39½" x 103"

■ Batting
78" x 103"

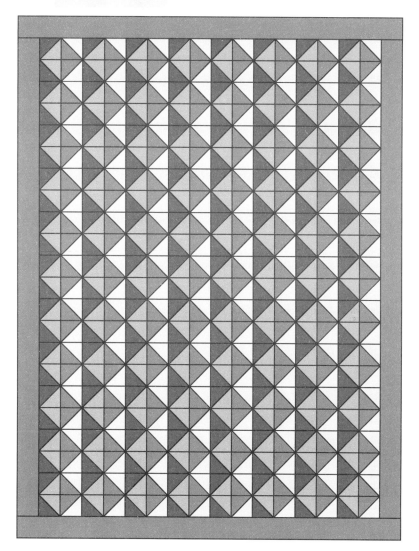

Diamond Shadows quilt
Block size: 8¼"
Quilt size: 74" x 98¾"
Set 8 x 11
Skill level: beginner

Assembly

1. Follow direction Nos. 1-2 in Diamond in a Whirl to make 88 blocks.

2. Sew 8 blocks together horizontally to make block row. Make 11 rows. Sew rows together.

3. Add side borders to either side of center panel; trim to fit. Add top and bottom borders; trim to fit.

4. Baste together top, batting, and lining. Quilt as desired. Bind to finish.

Snowball & Nine Patch

Snowball blocks can be combined with a variety of complementary blocks to make interesting designs. One common combination is with the simple Nine Patch block. A variation of this pattern featuring a Divided Nine Patch block is also given in two settings.

The center of the Snowball block (*Template 11*) must be cut from background fabric because it is too large to cut from a 5″ square. Using a background fabric also provides a necessary unifying factor for the scrap quilt. Be sure to cut these carefully so that grain line is correctly placed.

Snowball & Nine Patch quilt

Block size: 6″
Quilt size: 74″ x 98″
Set 11 x 15
Skill level: beginner

Materials

(40" fabric)

■ **5" Squares**
269 pieces
747 of *Template 2*
328 of *Template 4*

■ **Background fabric**
2⅝ yards
82 of *Template 11*

■ **Borders and binding**
2¾ yards
2 strips 4½" x 92½"
for sides
2 strips 4½" x 76½"
for top and bottom
binding strips
(2½" x 10 yards)

■ **Lining**
5⅝ yards
2 panels 40" x 102"

■ **Batting**
78" x 102"

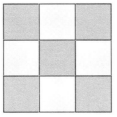

Nine Patch block

Snowball block

Piecing diagram

Piecing diagram

Assembly

1. Cut pieces as directed. Sew 3 *Template 2* patches together, alternating between light and dark squares. Join 3 of these rows together to make the Nine Patch block. Make 83 Nine Patch blocks.

2. Cut hexagons from background fabric, paying careful attention to the marked grain line. Add a triangle (*Template 4*) to each of the bias corners of the hexagon to make the Snowball block. Make 82 Snowball blocks.

3. Join 6 Nine Patch and 5 Snowball blocks, alternating types, to make 1 row. Make 8 rows of this type.

4. Join 6 Snowball and 5 Nine Patch blocks, alternating types, to make 1 row. Make 7 rows of this type. Referring to the quilt drawing, sew rows together, alternating types.

5. Add side borders to either side of center panel; trim to fit. Add top and bottom borders; trim to fit.

6. Baste together top, batting, and lining. Quilt as desired. Bind to finish.

Needle **Note**

All of the Snowball & Nine Patch quilts are easy to make in almost any size desired by adding or subtracting rows of blocks. The effect is most pleasing, however, when you use an odd number of rows as shown–11 x 15 or 7 x 9 , for instance.

Snowball & Divided Nine Patch

Snowball & Divided Nine Patch quilt Straight Furrows Setting

Block size: 6″

Quilt size: 50″ x 62″

Set 7 x 9

Skill level: intermediate

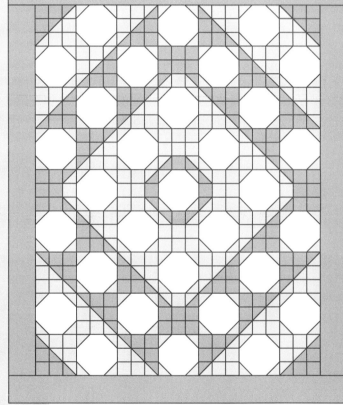

Snowball & Divided Nine Patch quilt Barn Raising Setting

Block size: 6″

Quilt size: 50″ x 62″

Set 7 x 9

Skill level: intermediate

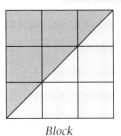

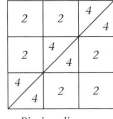

Unit 1

Block   Piecing diagram

Materials

(40" fabric)

■ 5" Squares
127 pieces
  192 of *Template 2*
  316 of *Template 4*

■ Background fabric
1¼ yards
  31 of *Template 11*

■ Borders and binding
1⅔ yards
  2 strips 4½" x 56½"
    for sides
  2 strips 4½" x 52½"
    for top and bottom
  binding strips
    (2½" x 6⅔ yards)

■ Lining
3 yards
  2 panels 34" x 54"

■ Batting
54" x 66"

Assembly

1. Make a Divided Nine Patch block by assembling 3 Unit 1s–a dark and a light triangle (*Template 4*) sewn together–3 dark squares (*Template 2*), and 3 light squares (*Template 2*). Assemble as shown in block drawing and piecing diagram. Make 32 Divided Nine Patch blocks.

2. Make 31 Snowball blocks as described in Snowball & Nine Patch direction No. 2 on page 91.

3. Join Divided Nine Patch and Snowball blocks, alternating types, to make block rows. Arrange blocks in the straight-furrows setting shown or anotherr variation of your choice. (The barn-raising setting shown requires 4 light and 4 dark transition blocks and only 24 of the regular Divided Nine Patch blocks. Refer to the quilt drawing to arrange blocks.)

4. Add side borders to either side of center panel; trim to fit. Add top and bottom borders; trim to fit.

5. Baste together top, batting, and lining. Quilt as desired. Bind to finish.

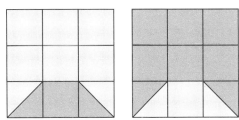

Transition blocks used for
barn-raising setting

Piecing diagram

Needle **Note**

The Divided Nine Patch block can be used in many settings. Because of its strong diagonal effect, it adapts easily to various Log Cabin sets. Transition blocks are given to create the barn-raising effect used in the quilt shown on opposite page.

Starlet

Because Starlet is a small block, it's suitable for small projects such as crib quilts. It's also a great pattern for using up the leftover fabric pieces from other projects. The points for each Starlet can be cut from one 5″ piece. You may wish to cut all the center squares from the same fabric to unify the quilt. Directions are given for a crib-size quilt project.

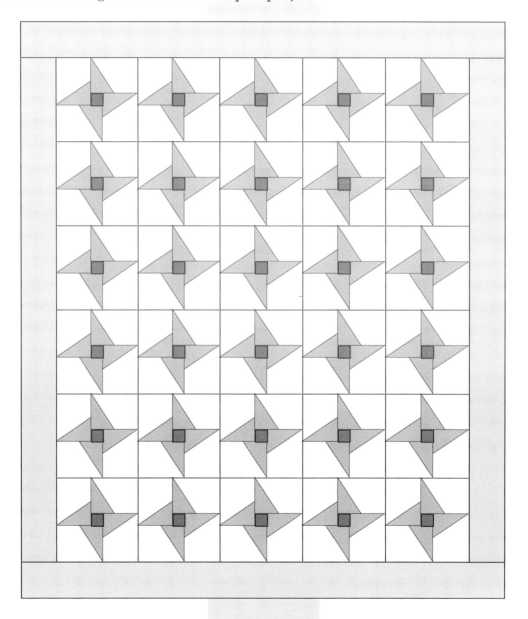

Starlet quilt
Block size: 7″
Quilt size: 43″ x 50″
Set 5 x 6
Skill level: beginner/intermediate

Materials

(40" fabric)

■ 5" Squares
30 pieces
120 of *Template 16*

■ Centers
⅛ yard
30 of *Template 17*

■ Background fabric
1⅓ yards
120 of *Template 35*

■ Borders and binding
1⅓ yards
2 strips 4½" x 44½"
for sides
2 strips 4½" x 45½"
for top and bottom
binding strips
(2½" x 5⅝ yards)

■ Lining
2⅔ yards
2 panels 28" x 47"

■ Batting
47" x 54"

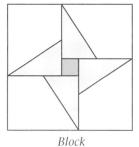
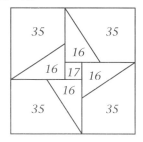
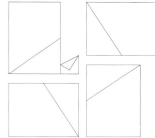

Block

Block piecing diagrams

Unit 1

Unit 1
piecing diagram

Assembly

1. Cut pieces as directed. Sew 4 Unit 1s containing patches from *Templates 16* and *35* for each block. Referring to piecing diagrams, make Starlet block by first sewing a partial seam of one unit to a *Template 17* piece. Add other units in turn, sewing in a counterclockwise direction, ending by finishing the partial open seam after adding the last unit. Make 30 blocks.

2. Join 5 blocks together in a horizontal row. Make 6 rows.

3. Add side borders to either side of center panel; trim to fit. Add top and bottom borders; trim to fit.

4. Baste together top, batting, and lining. Quilt as desired. Bind to finish.

Star Light, Star Bright

Star Light and Star Bright are companion blocks that alternate for a truly sparkling quilt. If you have made any other projects using pieces cut from *Templates 33, 34,* or *34-r,* you may already have leftover pieces that can be incorporated into this project.

The quilt is shown with a pieced border cut with *Template 3* from extra 5" squares. The quilt can be made larger or smaller by adding or subtracting blocks, but an odd-numbered setting (3 x 5, 5 x 7, etc.) shows these blocks off to their best advantage.

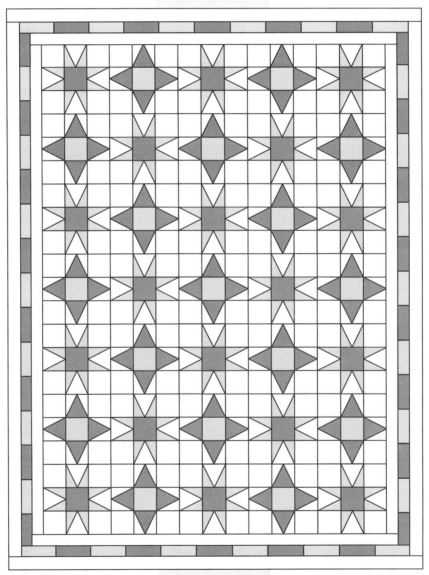

Star Light, Star Bright quilt
Block size: 11¼"
Quilt size: 68¼" x 90¾"
Set 5 x 7
Skill level: beginner/intermediate

Materials
(40" fabric)

■ **5" Squares**
133 pieces

    35 of *Template 12*

    68 of *Template 33*

    72 of *Template 34*

    72 of *Template 34-r*

    52 of *Template 3* for
      middle border

■ **Background, inner
border, outer border, and
binding**
5¼ yards

    140 of *Template 12*

    72 of *Template 3*

    68 of *Template 34*

    68 of *Template 34-r*

    2 strips 2½" x 81¼"
      for inner border sides

    2 strips 2½" x 62¾"
      for inner border top
      and bottom

    2 strips 2½" x 89¼"
      for outer border sides

    2 strips 2½" x 70¾"
      for outer border top
      and bottom

    binding strips
      (2½" x 9⅓ yards)

■ **Lining**
5⅓ yards

    2 panels 37" x 95"

■ **Batting**
73" x 95"

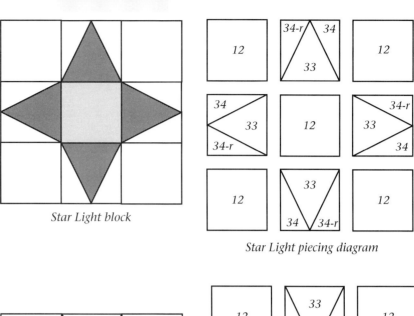

Star Light block

Star Light piecing diagram

Star Bright block

Star Bright piecing diagram

Assembly

1. Cut pieces as directed. Referring to the block drawings and piecing diagrams, make 17 Star Light blocks and 18 Star Bright blocks. Assemble 5 blocks alternately in horizontal rows; assemble rows into quilt top as shown in quilt drawing.

2. Add inner side borders to either side of center panel; trim to fit. Add top and bottom borders; trim to fit.

3. Piece 15 *Template 3* pieces together, following quilt drawing, for each middle border for the sides; piece 11 *Template 3* pieces together for each middle border for the top and bottom. Add these pieced borders; side borders first, top and bottom borders next.

4. Add outer borders to sides; trim to fit. Add outer top and bottom borders; trim to fit.

5. Baste together top, batting, and binding. Quilt as desired. Bind to finish.

Star Wreath

Star Wreath is a variation of the traditional 54-40 or Fight block. Arranging four of these blocks in a group as shown makes the wreath-like appearance of the four-block unit.

The colored squares cut from *Template 28* could be made a different color from the star points, or you might wish to choose the darkest of your 5" squares for the star points and make the squares from the lighter colors.

Any block that uses pieces cut from *Templates 34* and *34-r* creates a leftover piece from which *Template 33* can be cut. (See cutting diagram for *Templates 33, 34,* and *34-r* on page 140.) Two patterns in this book that will use those leftover pieces from *Template 33* are Windflower and Star Light.

The Christmas Wreath pattern is a two-color variation of this block and is found in the last section of the book with the scrap-cut quilt designs.

Star Wreath quilt
Block size: 11¼"
Quilt size: 58¼" x 82¾"
Set 4 x 6
Skill level: intermediate

Materials

(40" fabric)

■ 5" Squares
138 pieces

152 of *Template 28*
100 of *Template 34*
100 of *Template 34-r*

■ Background, sashing, borders, and binding
4½ yards

48 of *Template 12*
152 of *Template 28*
96 of *Template 33*
4 of *Template 34*
4 of *Template 34-r*
3 strips 2½" x 23"
  for vertical sashing
2 strips 2½" x 47½"
  for horizontal sashing
2 strips 6⅛" x 74"
  for sides
2 strips 6⅛" x 47½"
  for top and bottom
binding strips
  (2½" x 8⅓ yards)

■ Lining
4⅞ yards

2 panels 32" x 87"

■ Batting
62" x 87"

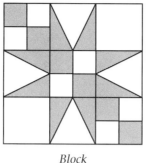

Block

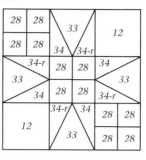

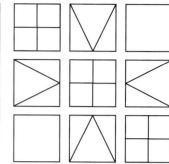

Piecing diagrams

Assembly

1. Cut pieces as directed. Referring to block drawing and piecing diagrams, make 24 blocks. Assemble these in groups of 4, rotating around the center as shown in the quilt drawing. Make 6 of these 4-block units.

2. Join 2 of these units together with a short vertical sash. Repeat for other 4 units.

3. Assemble quilt top by joining rows alternating with a long sashing strip, being careful to visually align short shashing strips.

4. Referring to corner-unit piecing diagram, make 4 quarter-block units for corners.

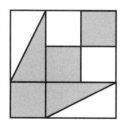

Quarter-block unit for corners

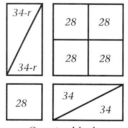

Quarter-block piecing diagram

5. Add side borders first; trim to fit. Measure top and bottom borders carefully, trim to fit and add corner blocks before sewing borders to the quilt top.

6. Baste together top, batting, and lining. Quilt as desired. Bind to finish.

Needle **Note**

If you cut your patches made from Templates 34 *and* 34-r *carefully, you will have enough wedge-shaped pieces (*Template 33*) left over to make another quilt top such as Windflower!*

Whirlagig

Cutting this block is very economical from a 5″ square because every bit of fabric is used. Two pairs of two contrasting fabric 5″ squares are used to make two blocks.

Because the block is asymmetrical, care must be taken that every piece is cut from the same side of the fabric. I cut all mine from the right side (see Whirlagig Garden on page 107). If you choose to do all your cutting from the wrong side of the fabric, the blocks will simply whirl in the other direction. Just be absolutely consistent!

The sashing arrangement for Whirlagig Garden is unusual in that it provides both the look of sashing and of a border without being one or the other. I chose to use all pastel floral fabrics in this quilt and was quite pleased with the results.

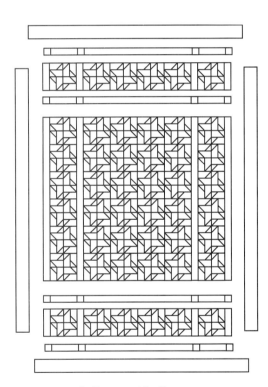

Quilt assembly diagram

Whirlagig Garden quilt

Block size: 7¾″

Quilt size: 62½″ x 78″

Set 6 x 8

Skill level: intermediate/advanced

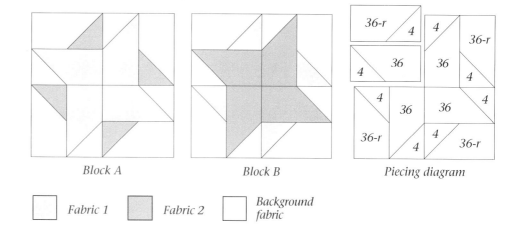

Block A Block B Piecing diagram

☐ Fabric 1 ▨ Fabric 2 ☐ Background fabric

Materials
(40" fabric)

■ 5" Squares
96 pieces
192 of *Template 4*
192 of *Template 36*

■ Background fabric
1⅞ yards
192 of *Template 4*
192 of *Template 36-r*

■ Sashing and binding
2⅓ yards
4 strips 2½" x 47"
4 strips 2½" x 31½"
16 strips 2½" x 8¼"
binding strips
(2½" x 8¼ yards)

■ Setting squares
⅛ yard
16 of *Template 2*

■ Borders
2⅛ yards
2 strips 4½" x 72½"
2 strips 4½" x 65"

■ Lining
4⅝ yards
2 panels 35" x 82"

■ Batting
66½" x 82"

Assembly

1. Sort your 5" fabric squares into pairs so that you have 2 squares in each of 2 fabrics as a set. Each set will make 2 blocks (Block A and Block B). Cut from each piece 2 each of *Templates 4* and *36*. (See cutting layout with *Template 36*.) Be sure that you cut with the same side of the fabric up every time.

2. Join these with background pieces cut from *Templates 4* and *36-r* as shown in the block drawings and piecing diagram to make blocks. Make 48 blocks, 24 each of Block A and Block B.

3. Sew 4 Block As together to make a block row. Make 6 block rows. Join rows together to make center panel.

4. Sew 2 sets of 6 Block Bs together vertically and add long sashing strips to either side. Sew these to either side of center panel, following quilt assembly diagram.

5. Make 16 *Template 2* setting squares. Sew 4 of these to 1 medium and 2 short sashing strips to make a sash row, following assembly diagram.

6. Sew 4 Block Bs together in a horizontal row. Make 2 rows. Add short sashing strips to either side of your remaining 4 Block Bs. Add these Block B units to either end of your Block B rows. Make 2 rows of this type. Sew a sashing row to the top and bottom of block rows, being careful to visually connect *Template 2* pieces to vertical sashing strips.

7. Add these 2 rows to the top and bottom of the center panel, following quilt assembly diagram, again piecing carefully to visually connect vertical sashing strips.

8. Add side borders to either side of quilt center; trim to fit. Add top and bottom borders; trim to fit.

9. Baste together top, batting, and lining. Quilt as desired. Bind to finish.

Windflower

Windflower is a charming pattern that will use up the wedge-shaped leftovers from projects like Anniversary Diamond, Star Wreath, and Star Tracks. (See cutting directions for *Templates 33, 34,* and *34-r* on page 140.)

The piecing is done with the around-the-square technique used on Starlet and is illustrated in the piecing diagram.

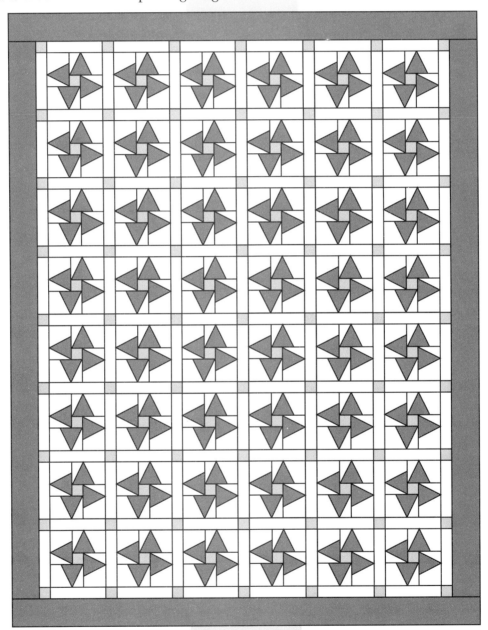

Windflower quilt
Block size: 9⅜"
Quilt size: 78¼" x 101"
Set 6 x 8
Skill level: intermediate

Materials
(40" fabric)

■ 5" Squares
192 pieces*
192 of *Template 33**

■ Accent fabric
⅝ yard
48 of *Template 28* for flower centers

63 of *Template 2* for setting squares

■ Background fabric
5⅓ yards
192 of *Template 22*
192 of *Template 34-r*
110 sashing strips 2½" x 9⅞"

■ Borders and binding
2⅞ yards
2 strips 4½" x 95½" for sides

2 strips 4½" x 80½" for top and bottom

binding strips (2½" x 10½ yards)

■ Lining
6⅞ yards
3 panels 36" x 82"

■ Batting
82" x 105"

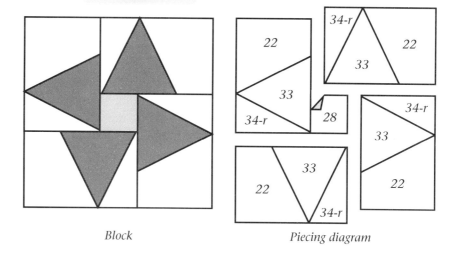

Block   Piecing diagram

Assembly

1. Cut pieces as directed. For each block assemble 4 Unit 1s using pieces cut from *Templates 22, 33,* and *34-r*. Attach 1 of these to a piece cut from *Template 28* by first sewing a partial seam, as shown in the piecing diagram. Attach each unit in turn, counter-clockwise, and finish sewing partial seam after last unit is attached. Make 48 blocks. *Note that setting squares and flower centers are very similar in size. Do not get them mixed up!*

2. Assemble horizontal block rows by alternating 6 blocks and 7 sashing strips. Make 8 block rows.

3. Make long sash rows by sewing together 7 *Template 2* pieces and 6 short sashing strips, alternating types. Make 9 sash rows. Join block rows and sash rows, alternating types.

4. Add side borders to either side of quilt center; trim to fit. Add top and bottom borders; trip to fit.

5. Baste together top, batting, and lining. Quilt as desired. Bind to finish.

Needle **Note**

* *Leftover wedge-shaped pieces from other projects in this book can be used to cut Template 33. For instance, if you have made the Anniversary Diamond quilt, you will have 200 of these leftover pieces.*

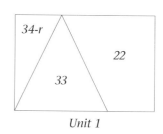

Unit 1

Zig Zag

Only one of the many possibilities of Zig Zag is illustrated here. Sort your 5" squares into darks and lights and cut into half diagonally (see directions for *Template 6*). Use *Template 23-r* for the light triangles and *Template 23* for the dark triangles. Arrange as shown to give the quilt a ridged illusion.

Materials
(40" fabric)

■ **5" Squares**
96 pieces
192 of *Template 6*

■ **Background fabric and binding**
4 yards
96 of *Template 23*
96 of *Template 23-r*
binding strips
(2½" x 6⅜ yards)

■ **Lining**
3 yards
2 panels 31" x 53½"

■ **Batting**
53½" x 61"

Block A   *Block B*

Block A piecing diagram   *Block B piecing diagram*

Zig Zag quilt
Block size: 4⅛" x 7⅛"
Quilt size: 49½" x 57"
Set 12 x 8
Skill level: beginner

Assembly

1. Sort your 5" squares into light and dark. Cut pieces as directed. Sew light triangles to accent pieces cut from *Template 23-r* to make Block A. Sew dark triangles to accent pieces cut from *Template 23* to make Block B. Make 96 blocks.

2. Starting with Block A as the first block, join 6 Block As with 6 Block Bs, alternating types. Make 8 rows. Sew rows together.

3. Baste together top, batting, and lining. Quilt as desired. Bind to finish.

Needle **Note**

No borders are shown on this quilt, but they may certainly be added to make it larger. Or you can make the quilt larger by increasing the number of 5" squares. Just remember that you will need more background fabric too! The ridged appearance will make it look something like a knitted afghan.

Cherry Vanilla

Mosaic I pattern (page 66), 30" x 30", machine pieced and machine quilted by the author, 1993.

Blueberry Ripple

Mosaic II pattern (page 70), 30" x 30", machine pieced and machine quilted by the author, 1993. Both of these quilts were made with scrap triangles. They are identical except for color and texture. The author wanted to demonstrate how much more vitality a quilt can appear to have when it is made from scrap pieces than when it has a more rigid color scheme.

Leigh's Snowball

Variation of the Snowball & Divided Nine Patch pattern, barn-raising setting, (page 92), 86½" x 100½", machine pieced and machine quilted by the author, 1992; from the collection of Leigh A. Simpson, Omaha, Nebraska. This variation on the Snowball & Nine Patch combination was created for the author's daughter and contains scraps in dark reds and medium pinks. The barn-raising setting uses "transition" blocks at the corners of the design to help it continue smoothly around the center.

Whirlagig Garden

Whirlagig pattern (page 100), 62½" x 78", machine pieced and machine quilted by the author, 1993. According to Doreen, this quilt was fun to make because of the process of matching the pairs of fabric to make the Whirlagigs. The fabrics chosen were selected from medium-size flower prints combined with smaller flower prints. Few quilts have contained so many different flower prints, but it works. The sashing was limited so that it framed but did not dominate the quilt.

Christmas Welcome

Variation of the Christmas Wreath pattern (page 98), 30" x 81", machine pieced and hand quilted by Jean Hay, Melrose, Massachusetts, 1994. Jean used only three of the Christmas Wreath blocks and stacked them in a vertical row to make this Christmas banner that welcomes visitors to the Christmas caroling party that she and her husband, Gerry Molina, host annually.

Sparkler

Anniversary Diamond, pieced border option, pattern (page 117), 37½" x 37½", machine pieced and machine quilted by the author, 1993. This small wall hanging was created especially to show how the green leftovers cut from the 5" charm pieces could be used to make a border.
Quilters never waste anything!

Southwestern Stars

Variation of the Friendship Star pattern (page 120), *62" x 74", machine pieced and machine quilted by Beth Meek, Windham, New Hampshire, 1994. The bright colors of the blocks were drawn together by the vivid Southwestern print Beth chose for the border. For her inner borders Beth used up leftover pieces from a 5" die-cut squares packet.

Almost Amish

Variation of the Scrap Star pattern (page 82), 42" x 42", machine pieced and
machine quilted by Jean Hay, Melrose, Massachusetts, 1994. The dark
background makes a nice contrast for the solid colors used in this wall
hanging, giving an "almost Amish" flavor to the piece. Jean varied the quilt
from the pattern by adding sash rows to set the blocks apart.

Star Tracks

Star Tracks pattern (page 130), 39¼" x 39¼", machine pieced and machine quilted by the author, 1993. The vivid colors of these stars are set off by a pinkish watercolor background. The placement of colors is quite carefully arranged and balanced. The author prefers multi-fabric quilts that are carefully planned so that the many fabrics lend interest but do not lead to chaos.

Jewel Box

Variation of the Twill Weave pattern (page 134), 58" x 77", machine pieced and hand quilted by Moira Clegg, Windham, New Hampshire, 1994. Bright colors, intricately woven give this very simple block a much more complex look.

Scrap-cut Quilts

The quilt designs that follow are created to use two different color families of 5″ squares. While any of them can be made by substituting a background fabric for the second color, the range of fabric possibilities with two color families makes these quilts more exciting. In most cases they require pieces with a strong color contrast, so white prints are a good selection for one of the colors.

Anniversary Diamond

Anniversary Diamond is an easier version of the traditional Double Wedding Ring block because it has no curved pieces. This block requires two colors. I used pastel green and pink in the wall hanging I made, then because that looked anemic to me, I added a really strong background fabric. Because the piece was small, I used up the leftover wedge-shaped pieces in a pieced border that is entirely optional. Measurements are also given for square borders.

The Anniversary Diamond quilt was planned as a companion quilt for Windflower. Each uses the pieces left over from the other. (See cutting directions for *Templates 33, 34,* and *34-r* on page 140.)

Anniversary Diamond quilt
Block size: 15"
Quilt size: 83" x 87"
Set 5 x 5
Skill level: intermediate

Materials
(40" fabric)

■ 5" Squares
(color 1, indicated by dark)
200 pieces
 200 of *Template 34*
 200 of *Template 34-r*

■ 5" Squares
(color 2, indicated by light)
150 pieces
 200 of *Template 28*
 100 of *Template 12*

■ Background fabric
(color 3, indicated by white)
3⅛ yards
 100 of *Template 28*
 25 of *Template 12*
 100 of *Template 33*
 100 of *Template 34*
 100 of *Template 34-r*

■ Borders and binding
2½ yards
 2 strips 4½" x 77½"
  for sides
 2 strips 6½" x 85½"
  for top and bottom
 binding strips
  (2½" x 10 yards)

■ Lining
7½ yards
 3 panels 31" x 87"

■ Batting
87" x 91"

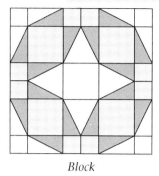

Block

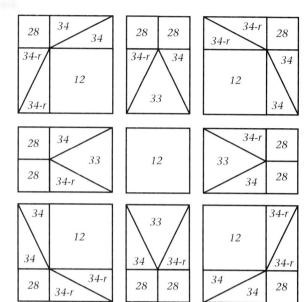

Piecing diagram

Assembly

1. Cut pieces as directed. Follow cutting directions carefully for *Templates 34* and *34-r* if you wish to have leftover pieces to make another project such as Windflower.

2. Make 25 blocks as shown in the piecing diagram. Assemble blocks into 5 horizontal rows of 5 blocks each. Sew rows together to make top.

3. Add side borders to either side of center panel; trim to fit. Add top and bottom borders; trim to fit.

4. Baste together top, batting, and lining. Quilt as desired. Bind to finish.

Anniversary Diamond

Materials
(40" fabric)

■ **5" Squares**
(color 1, indicated by dark)
32 pieces
   32 of *Template 34*
   32 of *Template 34-r*

■ **5" Squares**
(color 2, indicated by light)
24 pieces
   32 of *Template 28*
   16 of *Template 12*

■ **Background and binding**
(color 3, indicated by white)
1 yard
   16 of *Template 28*
   4 of *Template 12*
   16 of *Template 33*
   16 of *Template 34*
   16 of *Template 34-r*
   binding strips
     (2½" x 4½ yards)

■ **Inner borders**
¼ yard
   2 strips 1½" x 32½"
     for sides
   2 strips 1½" x 34½"
     for top and bottom

■ **Outer borders**
⅓ yard
   2 strips 2½" x 34½"
     for sides
   2 strips 2½" x 38½"
     for top and bottom

■ **Lining**
1¼ yards
   1 panel 40" x 40"

■ **Batting**
40" x 40"

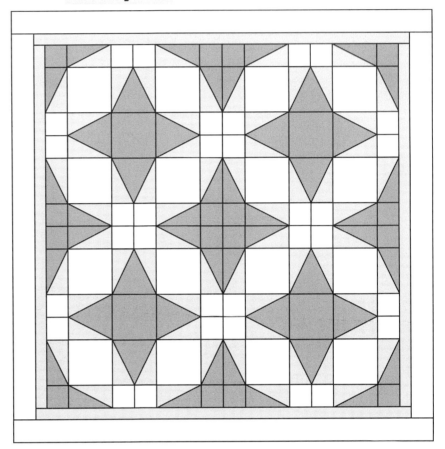

Anniversary Diamond wall hanging
Block size: 15"
Quilt size: 36" x 36"
Set 2 x 2
Skill level: beginner/intermediate

Assembly

1. Cut pieces as directed. Make 4 blocks as shown in piecing diagram on page 115. Sew blocks together.

2. Add inner side borders to either side of center panel; trim to fit. Add inner top and bottom borders; trim to fit. Add outer side borders; trim to fit. Add outer top and bottom borders; trim to fit.

3. Baste together top, batting, and lining. Quilt as desired. Bind to finish.

Anniversary Diamond

Border Materials

(40" fabric)

Border uses leftover pieces from the qulit top.

■ 5" Squares

(color 1, indicated by dark)

36 of *Template 33*
(32 of these are the pieces you have leftover from cutting *Templates 34* and *34-r* for the quilt top. You will need to cut an additional 4 of *Template 33* for the border.)

4 of *Template 32*
(You need these only if you wish to make corners square.)

■ Background fabric

(color 2, indicated by light)

½ yard

32 of *Template 33*

4 of *Template 37*

binding strips
(2½" x 4⅔ yards)

■ Lining

2⅓ yards

■ Batting

42" x 42"

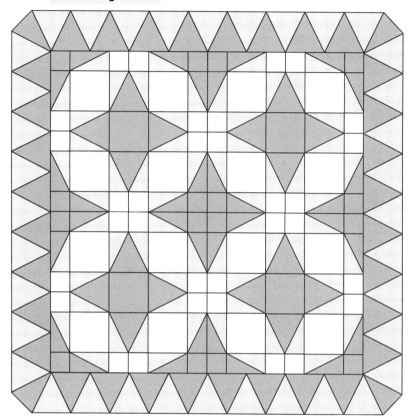

Pieced Border Option

Quilt size: 37½" x 37½"

Set 2 x 2

Assembly

1. Follow directions for Anniversary Diamond wall hanging, except for borders.

2. Assemble pieced borders in strips, adding a *Template 37* to each end of the top and bottom strips. Attach as shown in *Fig. 1*. If you wish to make square corners on the wall hanging, add *Template 32* to each corner (*Fig. 2*).

3. Baste together top, batting, and lining. Quilt as desired. Bind to finish.

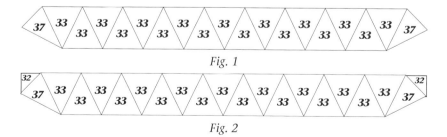

Christmas Wreath

Christmas Wreath is a variation of Star Wreath (page 98), and both are variants of the traditional 54-40 or Fight block. Made up in reds and greens as a wall hanging, it will make a pretty seasonal accent for your home.

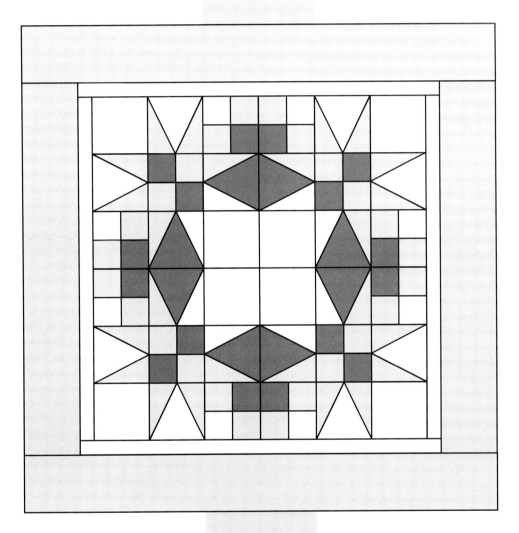

Christmas Wreath wall hanging

Block size: 11¼"

Quilt size: 32½" x 32½"

Set 2 x 2

Skill level: beginner/intermediate

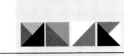

Materials

(40" fabric)

■ 5" Squares

(green, indicated by light color)
18 pieces
  24 of *Template 28*
  12 of *Template 34*
  12 of *Template 34-r*

■ 5" Squares

(red, indicated by dark color)
12 pieces
  16 of *Template 28*
  8 of *Template 33*

■ Background and inner border

⅝ yard
  8 of *Template 12*
  8 of *Template 28*
  8 of *Template 33*
  4 of *Template 34*
  4 of *Template 34-r*
  2 strips 1½" x 23"
    for sides
  2 strips 1½" x 25"
    for top and bottom

■ Outer border and binding

⅞ yard
  2 strips 4½" x 27"
    for sides
  2 strips 4½" x 35"
    for top and bottom
  binding strips
    (2½" x 4⅛ yards)

■ Lining

1⅛ yards

■ Batting

37" x 37"

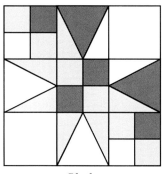

Block

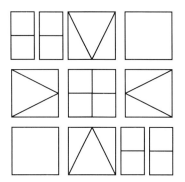 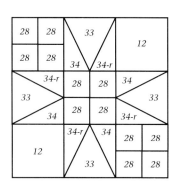

Piecing diagrams

Assembly

1. Cut pieces as directed. Make 4 blocks as shown in piecing diagram. Referring to quilt drawing, sew 4 blocks together, rotating round the center.

2. Add inner side borders to either side of center panel; trim to fit. Add inner top and bottom borders; trim to fit. Add outer side borders; trim to fit. Add outer top and bottom borders; trim to fit.

3. Baste together top, batting, and lining. Quilt as desired. Bind to finish.

Friendship Star

Friendship Star makes a nice contrast with itself when the blocks are made from two different color families of 5″ squares. These need to offer a strong contrast with each other to create the checkerboard effect shown in the quilt drawing.

Friendship Star quilt

Block size: 12⅜″
Quilt size: 57½″ x 82¼″
Set 4 x 6
Skill level: beginner

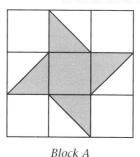
Block A

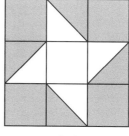
Block B

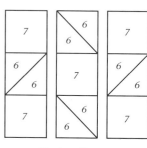
Piecing diagram

Materials

(40" fabric)

■ 5" Squares
(color 1, indicated by dark)
108 pieces
   96 of *Template 6*
   60 of *Template 7*

■ 5" Squares
(color 2, indicated by white)
108 pieces
   96 of *Template 6*
   60 of *Template 7*

■ *Borders and binding*
2¼ yards
   2 strips 4½" x 76¾"
      for sides
   2 strips 4½" x 60"
      for top and bottom
   binding strips
      (2½" x 8⅓ yards)

■ *Lining*
5 yards
   2 panels 32" x 87"

■ *Batting*
62" x 87"

Assembly

1. Cut pieces as directed. Referring to block drawings and piecing diagram, make 12 each of Block A and Block B.

2. Join 2 Block As and 2 Block Bs, alternating types according to quilt drawing, to make a block row. Make 6 block rows.

3. Add side borders to either side of center panel; trim to fit. Add top and bottom borders; trim to fit.

4. Baste together top, batting, and lining. Quilt as desired. Bind to finish.

Needle **Note**

Because of its name, this quilt could make a fine friendship quilt or a gift for a special friend. Names and special messages could be embroidered or inked in the block centers, or only in the lighter centers of Block B.

Kitten Chow

The traditional Puss in the Corner block in a two-color combination gives a sort of "Ralston Purina" look to this quilt, therefore the name Kitten Chow. If you can find one of the delightful fabrics printed with cats for the borders, the association would be even stronger.

Kitten Chow quilt
Block size: 8½"
Quilt size: 59" x 76"
Set 6 x 8
Skill level: beginner

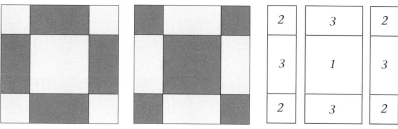

Block A   Block B   Piecing diagram

Materials

(40" fabric)

■ 5" Squares

(color 1, indicated by light)

96 pieces

24 of *Template 1*
96 of *Template 2*
96 of *Template 3*

■ 5" Squares

(color 2, indicated by dark)

96 pieces

24 of *Template 1*
96 of *Template 2*
96 of *Template 3*

■ Borders and binding

2⅛ yards

2 strips 4½" x 70½"
    for sides
2 strips 4½" x 61½"
    for top and bottom
binding strips
    (2½" x 8 yards)

■ Lining

3½ yards

2 panels 40" x 63"

■ Batting

63" x 80"

Assembly

1. Cut pieces as directed. Make 24 Block As with corners and center in color 1 prints (light); make 24 Block Bs with corners and center in color 2 prints (dark).

2. Alternating Blocks A and B, make horizontal rows of 6 blocks. Make 8 rows. Assemble rows into quilt top.

3. Add side borders to either side of center panel; trim to fit. Add top and bottom borders; trim to fit.

4. Baste together top, batting, and lining. Quilt as desired. Bind to finish.

Links

Links uses two different color families of 5″ pieces quite effectively. These are referred to as dark and light fabrics for convenience only. You will need a few more than 100 pieces of each.

Organize the quilt so that one color is arranged horizontally and one vertically. The background fabric chosen should offer a good contrast to both colors, and the effect should be of interwoven ribbons. You may wish to shade the blocks from dark to light.

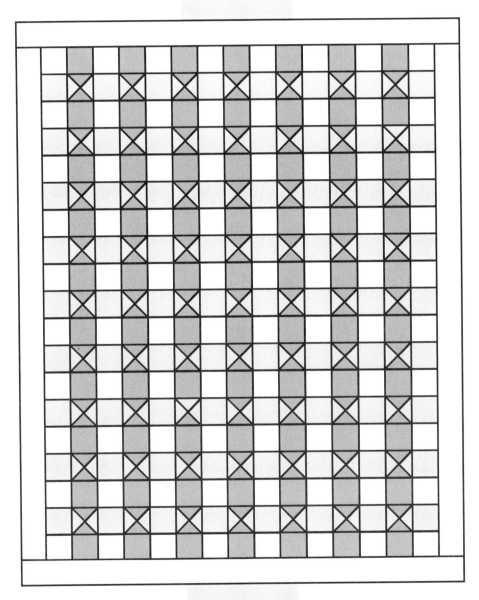

Links quilt
Block size: 3¾″
Quilt size: 64¼″ x 79¼″
Set 15 x 19
Skill level: beginner

Materials

(40" fabric)

■ 5" Squares

(color 1, indicated by dark)
102 pieces
126 of *Template 5*
70 of *Template 12*

■ 5" Squares

(color 2, indicated by light)
104 pieces
126 of *Template 5*
72 of *Template 12*

■ Background, borders, and binding

(color 3, indicated by white)
2¼ yards
80 of *Template 12*
2 strips 4½" x 73¾"
for sides
2 strips 4½" x 66¾"
for top and bottom
binding strips
(2½" x 8½ yards)

■ Lining

4⅝ yards
2 panels 34½" x 83¼"

■ Batting

68¼" x 83¼"

Block A

Block B

Block C

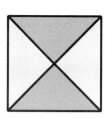
Block D

*Block A, B, & C
piecing diagram*

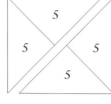
*Block D
piecing diagram*

Assembly

1. Cut patches as directed, making 72 Block As, 70 Block Bs, 80 Block Cs, and 63 Block Ds.

2. Sew together 8 Block As and 7 Block Bs alternately to make block row. Make 10 block rows of this type.

3. Sew together 8 Block Cs and 7 Block Ds alternately to make block row. Make 9 block rows of this type. Join block rows, alternating types.

4. Add side borders to either side of quilt; trim to fit. Add top and bottom borders; trim to fit.

5. Layer quilt top with batting and lining and baste. Quilt as desired. Bind to finish.

Ribbons in the Breeze

The arrangement of the blocks in this quilt makes it look like a quilt set on the diagonal, but it's not! Fluttering ribbons and twirling pinwheels give this quilt movement and excitement. By taking your time and following the quilt drawing closely for color placement, you'll find this quilt is not quite as difficult to piece as it first appears.

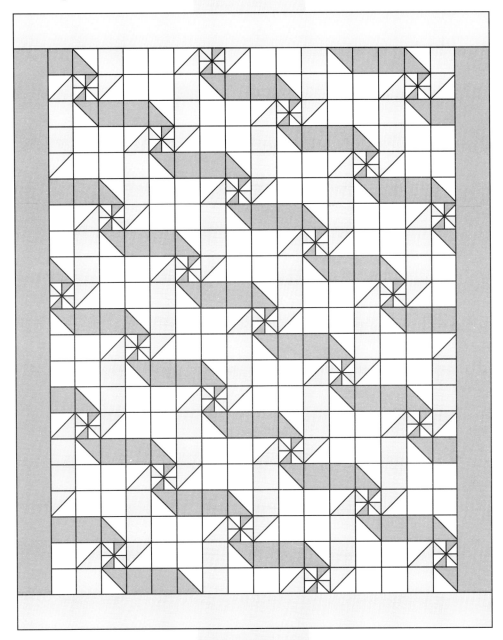

Ribbons in the Breeze quilt
Block size: 4"

Quilt size: 72" x 92"

Set 16 x 21

Skill level: intermediate

Block A

Block B

Block C

Block D

Block E

Block F

*Piecing diagram
for Blocks D & E*

*Piecing diagram
for Block F*

Materials

(40" fabric)

■ 5" Squares

(color 1, indicated by dark)

91 pieces

52 of *Template 4*
52 of *Template 8*
52 of *Template 9*

■ 5" Squares

(color 2, indicated by light)

91 pieces

52 of *Template 4*
52 of *Template 8*
52 of *Template 9*

■ Background fabric

3⅛ yards

104 of *Template 4*
102 of *Template 8*
104 of *Template 9*

■ Side borders

(to coordinate with color 1)

2⅝ yards*

2 strips 4½" x 86½"
for sides*

■ Top and bottom borders and binding

2¼ yards*

(to coordinate with color 2)

2 strips 4½" x 74½"
for top and bottom*
binding strips
(2½" x 9⅝ yards)

■ Lining

5⅛ yards

2 panels 39" x 96"

■ Batting

76" x 96"

Assembly

1. Cut pieces as directed. Make 102 Block As, 52 Block Bs, 52 Block Cs, 52 Block Ds, 52 Block Es, and 26 Block Fs. Be sure that pinwheels in Block F are turning in the right direction.

2. Following quilt drawing carefully, make the quilt top by constructing horizontal rows of these blocks, noting the direction each pieced block is turned. Make 21 rows. Join rows together following quilt drawing to make the top.

3. Add side borders to either side of center panel; trim to fit. Add top and bottom borders; trim to fit.

4. Baste together top, batting, and lining. Quilt as desired. Bind to finish.

Needle **Note**

*If all four borders and binding are made from the same fabric, you'll need only 2⅝ total yards of fabric. This will save you 2¼ yards of fabric!

Snowball Cross

Snowball Cross requires two color families that have very strong color contrast. There is no background fabric, so use white prints to serve that purpose. This quilt will look best if setting is by odd numbers–3 x 5, 5 x 7, etc. The size given is suitable for a lap quilt.

The hexagon unit is made by a "connecting-up" method popularized by MaryEllen Hopkins, and the hexagon piece itself is created from a 5″ square with no cutting beforehand. Practice sewing on the diagonal with no marking by watching where your needle is headed, not where it is.

Snowball Cross quilt
Block size: 13½″
Quilt size: 49½″ x 76½″
Set 3 x 5
Skill level: beginner

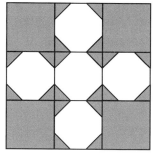
Block A

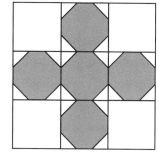
Block B

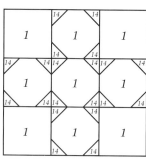
Piecing diagram

Materials
(40" fabric)

■ 5" Squares
(color 1, indicated by dark)
107 pieces

> 75 of *Template 1* (32 for background block square; 35 for Snowball centers)
>
> 160 of *Template 14*

■ 5" Squares
(color 2, indicated by white)
103 pieces

> 68 of *Template 1* (28 for background block square; 40 for Snowball centers)
>
> 140 of *Template 14*

■ Borders and binding
2⅛ yards

> 2 strips 5" x 70" for sides
>
> 2 strips 5" x 52" for top and bottom
>
> binding strips (2½" x 7½ yards)

■ Lining
4½ yards

> 2 panels 28" x 81"

■ Batting
54" x 81"

Assembly

1. Cut pieces as directed. Make hexagon units by the connecting-up method shown with *Template 14* (page 138).

2. Following block drawings and piecing diagram, make 8 Block As and 7 Block Bs.

3. Referring to quilt diagram, sew together blocks in rows of 3, alternating types. Make 5 rows. Join rows.

4. Add side borders to either side of center panel; trim to fit. Add top and bottom borders; trim to fit.

5. Baste together top, batting, and lining. Quilt as desired. Bind to finish.

Needle **Note**

If you wish to piece the Snowball blocks in the traditional manner, use Template 10 (page 140) for the hexagon and Template 4 for the corner triangles. Cut 32 Template 1, 35 of Template 10, and 160 of Template 4 from color 1. Cut 28 of Template 1, 40 of Template 10, and 140 of Template 4 from color 2.

Star Tracks

Star Tracks is a variation on the traditional 54-40 or Fight block. The wall hanging features the block set on point and pieced setting triangles. These features combine to make this a very attractive quilt.

Star Tracks is one of the blocks that can be used as a companion block to Windflower because its *Templates 34* and *34-r* leave a leftover piece (*Template 33*) suitable for use in Windflower.

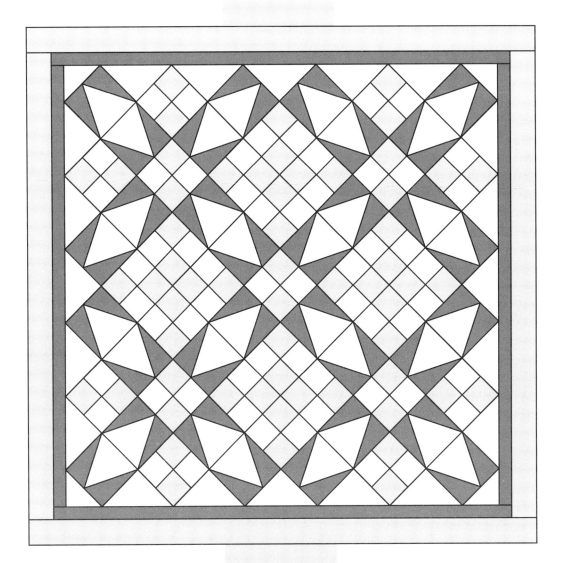

Star Tracks wall hanging
Block size: 11¾"
Quilt size: 39¼" x 39¼"
Set 2 x 2 (on point)
Skill level: beginner/intermediate

Materials

(40" fabric)

■ **5" Squares**

(color 1, indicated by dark)
28 pieces
- 28 of *Template 34*
- 28 of *Template 34-r*

■ **5" Squares**

(color 2, indicated by light)
12 pieces
- 48 of *Template 28*

■ **Background fabric**

(color 3, indicated by white)
1 yard
- 48 of *Template 28*
- 4 of *Template 5* (note different grain line and cut accordingly)
- 28 of *Template 33*
- 20 of *Template 38* (note different grain line and cut accordingly)

■ **Inner border**

¼ yard
- 2 strips 1½" x 35¾" for sides
- 2 strips 1½" x 37¾" for top and bottom

■ **Outer border and binding**

1¼ yards
- 2 strips 2½" x 37¾" for sides
- 2 strips 2½" x 41¾" for top and bottom
- binding strips (2½" x 5 yards)

■ **Lining**

2½ yards
- 2 panels 22" x 42"

■ **Batting**

44" x 44"

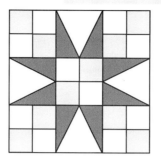

Block

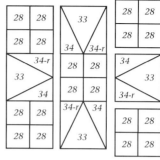

Piecing diagram 1

Unit 1

Unit 2

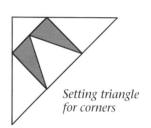

Setting triangle for sides

Setting triangle for corners

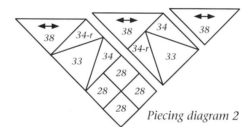

Piecing diagram 2

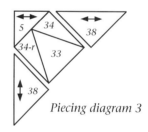

Piecing diagram 3

Assembly

1. Cut pieces as directed. Note grain line on all templates, especially *Templates 5* and *38*. (*Template 5* in this project only has a grain line different from that marked on the regular template.)

2. Make 5 Unit 1s and 4 Unit 2s. Sew units together in rows of 3, alternating types as shown in piecing diagram 1, to make block.

3. Make 4 large setting triangles for the sides as shown in piecing diagram 2, and 4 setting triangles for corners as shown in piecing diagram 3.

4. Assemble quilt top diagonally as shown in general directions.

5. Add inner side borders to either side of center panel; trim to fit. Add inner top and bottom borders; trim to fit. Add outer side borders; trim to fit. Add outer top and bottom borders; trim to fit.

6. Baste together top, batting, and lining. Quilt as desired. Bind to finish.

Tinker Toys

Two color families invoke the image of the familiar children's toy. The easy-to-make Snowball blocks are created by sewing on the diagonal – see the instructions with *Templates 10* and *14* (pages 138 and 140). This quilt can be made larger or smaller by adding rows of blocks or partial blocks. It's a great pattern for making a quick-and-easy crib quilt.

Tinker Toys quilt
Block size: 4½"

Quilt size: 58½" x 76½"

Set 11 x 15

Skill level: beginner

Materials

(40" fabric)

■ 5" Squares

(color 1, indicated by dark)
117 pieces
> 164 of *Template 26*
> 140 of *Template 14*

■ 5" Squares

(color 2, indicated by light)
76 pieces
> 82 of *Template 26*
> 35 of *Template 1* (for
> Snowball patch)

■ Background fabric

(color 3, indicated by white)
⅞ yard
> 48 of *Template 1* for Block C

■ Borders and binding

2⅛ yards
> 2 strips 5" x 70" for sides
> 2 strips 5" x 61" for top
>   and bottom
> binding strips
>   (2½" x 8 yards)

■ Lining

4½ yards
> 2 panels 32" x 81"

■ Batting

63" x 81"

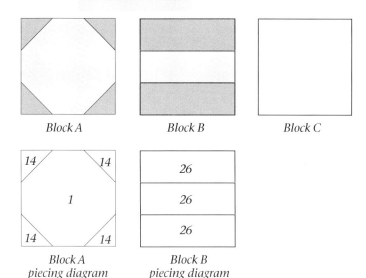

Block A   *Block B*   *Block C*

Block A   *Block B*
piecing diagram *piecing diagram*

Assembly

1. Cut pieces as directed. Make 35 Block As (make hexagon units by the connecting-up method shown with *Template 14* on page 138), 82 Block Bs, and 48 Block Cs, as shown in the block drawings and piecing diagrams.

2. Join 6 Block Cs with 5 Block Bs, alternating types. Refer to the quilt diagram for the correct orientation of Block B. Make 8 block rows of this type.

3. Join 6 Block Bs with 5 Block As, alternating types. Refer to the quilt diagram for the correct orientation of Block B. Make 7 block rows of this type.

4. Referring to the quilt diagram, join block rows, alternating types.

5. Add side borders to either side of center panel; trim to fit. Add top and bottom borders; trim to fit.

6. Baste together top, batting, and lining. Quilt as desired. Bind to finish.

Twill Weave

Materials

(40" fabric)

■ **5" Squares**
(color 1, indicated by dark)
120 pieces
    240 of *Template 3*

■ **5" Squares**
(color 2, indicated by light)
120 pieces
    240 of *Template 3*

■ **Background, borders, and binding**
(color 3, indicated by white)
2⅝ yards
    120 of *Template 13*
    2 strips 4½" x 80½"
        for sides
    2 strips 4½" x 75½"
        for top and bottom
    binding strips
        (2½" x 9⅓ yards)

■ **Lining**
5 yards
    2 panels 39" x 90"

■ **Batting**
77" x 90"

Although Twill Weave is made with easy-to-cut pieces, it has a very complex appearance. The piecing technique is a useful one to learn because it can be used in many situations where you might otherwise have an inset seam.

Twill Weave quilt

Block size: 6½"

Quilt size: 73" x 86"

Set 10 x 12

Skill level:
beginner/intermediate

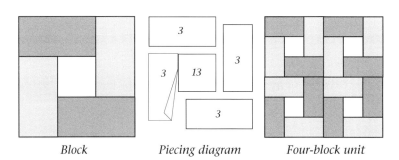

Block   *Piecing diagram*   *Four-block unit*

Needle Note

The background fabric chosen should offer a good strong contrast to both colors in the block.

Assembly

1. Cut pieces as directed. Make 120 blocks following piecing diagram. Sew partial seam first, and add *Template 3* pieces in turn. The last seam will complete the first partial seam. Be careful to always start with the same color and on the same side. It is possible to make this block into its own mirror image if you are not careful.

2. Sew blocks into 30 groups of 4, rotating around the center as shown in the 4-block Unit diagram. Sew 5 of these multi-block units together to make 6 horizontal rows. Sew rows together.

3. Add side borders to either side of center panel; trim to fit. Add top and bottom borders; trim to fit.

4. Baste together top, batting, and lining. Quilt as desired. Bind to finish.

Templates

Templates for this book are shown with ¼" seam allowances. Small cutting diagrams show the best way to cut templates from 5" pre-cut squares. Some templates are easy to cut without the use of templates by following directions given with the diagrams.

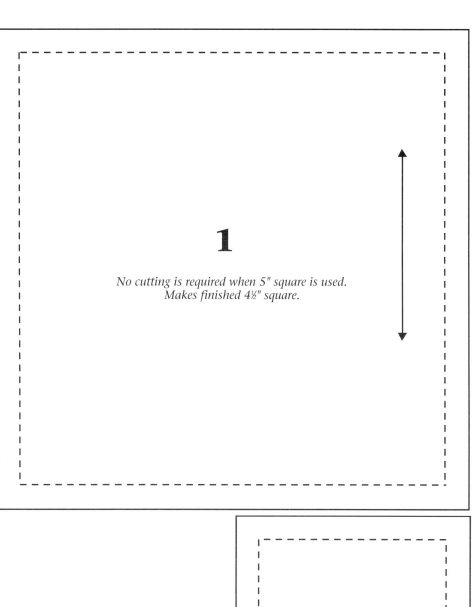

1

*No cutting is required when 5" square is used.
Makes finished 4½" square.*

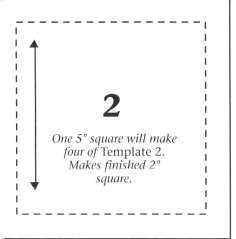

2

One 5" square will make four of Template 2. *Makes finished 2" square.*

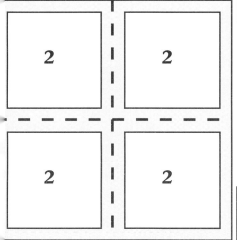

Cutting diagram for Template 2–*Cut 2½" from sides, both horizontally and vertically.*

Cutting diagram for Template 3–*Measure 2½" from one edge, and cut square in half. Makes two finished rectangles 2" x 4½".*

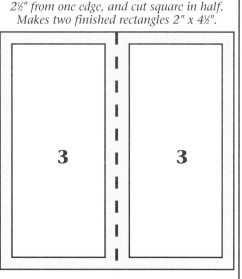

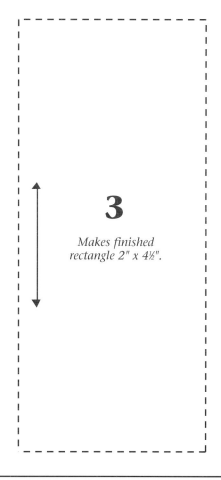

3

Makes finished rectangle 2" x 4½".

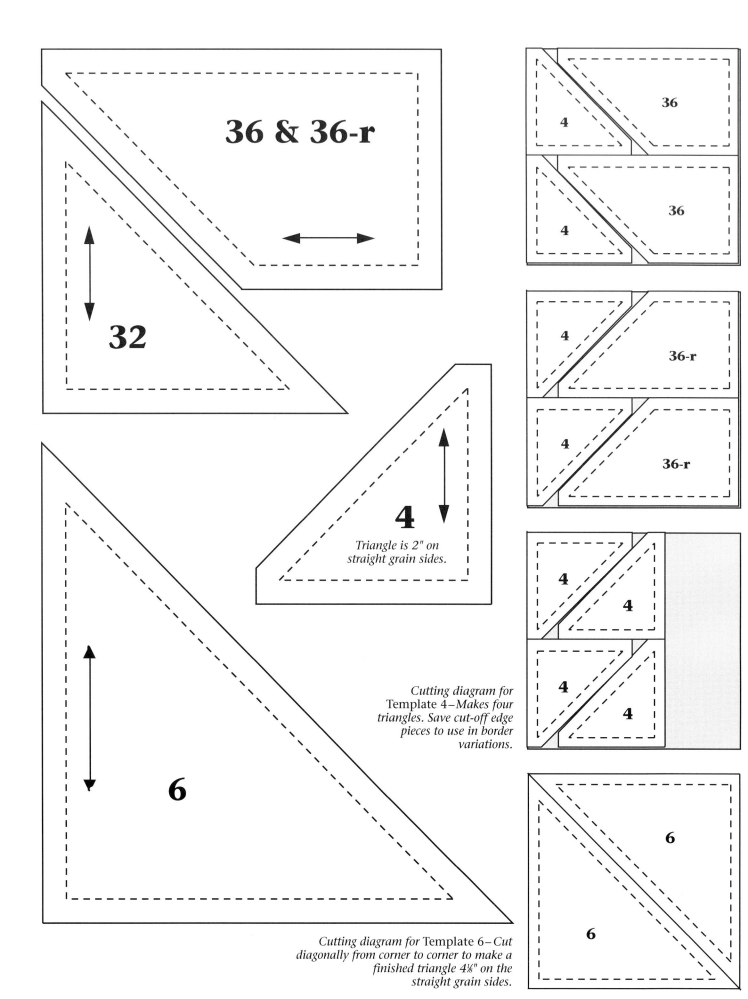

36 & 36-r

32

4

Triangle is 2" on straight grain sides.

6

36

36

4

4

4

36-r

4

36-r

4

4

4

4

Cutting diagram for Template 4–Makes four triangles. Save cut-off edge pieces to use in border variations.

6

6

Cutting diagram for Template 6– Cut diagonally from corner to corner to make a finished triangle 4⅛" on the straight grain sides.

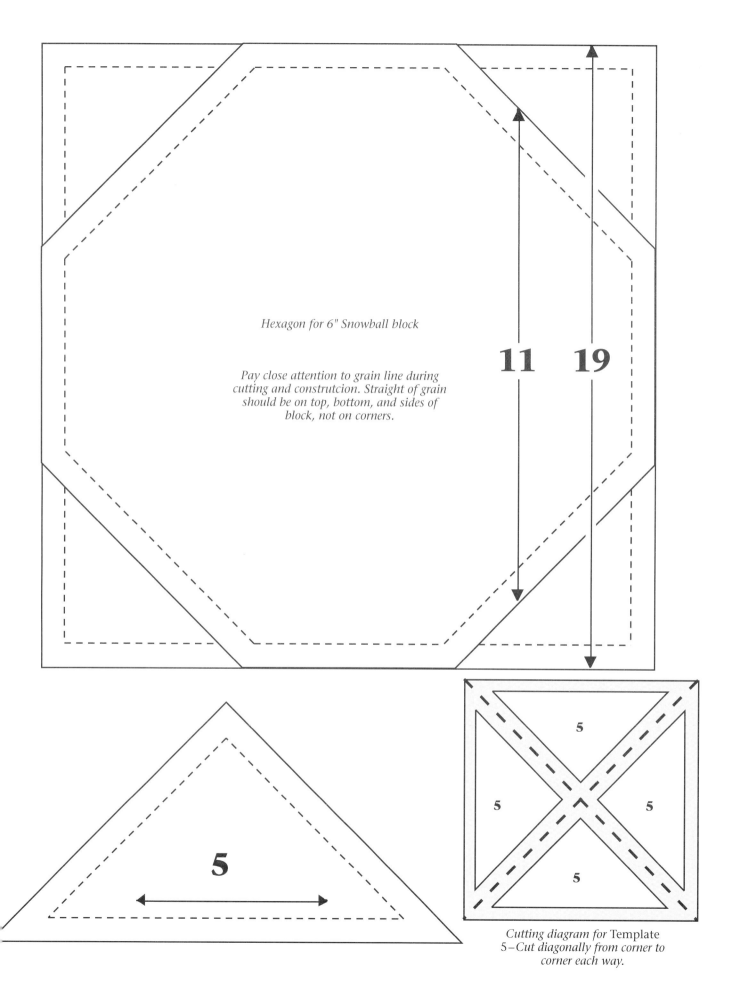

Hexagon for 6" Snowball block

Pay close attention to grain line during cutting and construtcion. Straight of grain should be on top, bottom, and sides of block, not on corners.

11 19

5

5

5   5

5

Cutting diagram for Template 5–Cut diagonally from corner to corner each way.

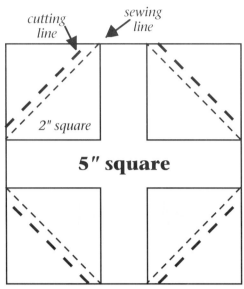

cutting line

sewing line

2" square

5" square

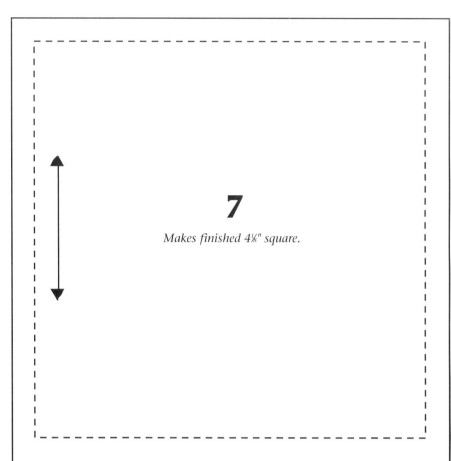

7

Makes finished 4⅛" square.

To make 4½" Snowball block from 5" squares without using templates, apply 2" square to each corner of 5" square, sewing across diagonal as shown, to make corner triangles. Trim to ¼" seam allownaces and press back corners to make 4½" Snowball block.

14

2" square for making no-template 4½" Snowball block.

No seam allowances are added.

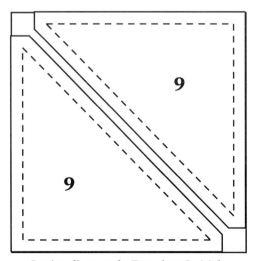

9

9

Cutting diagram for Template 9—Makes finished triangles 4" on the straight-grain side.

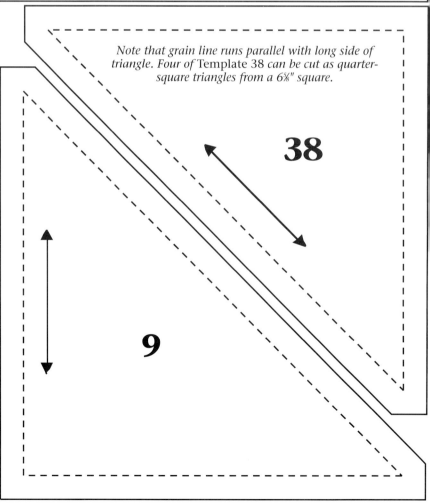

Note that grain line runs parallel with long side of triangle. Four of Template 38 can be cut as quarter-square triangles from a 6⅜" square.

38

9

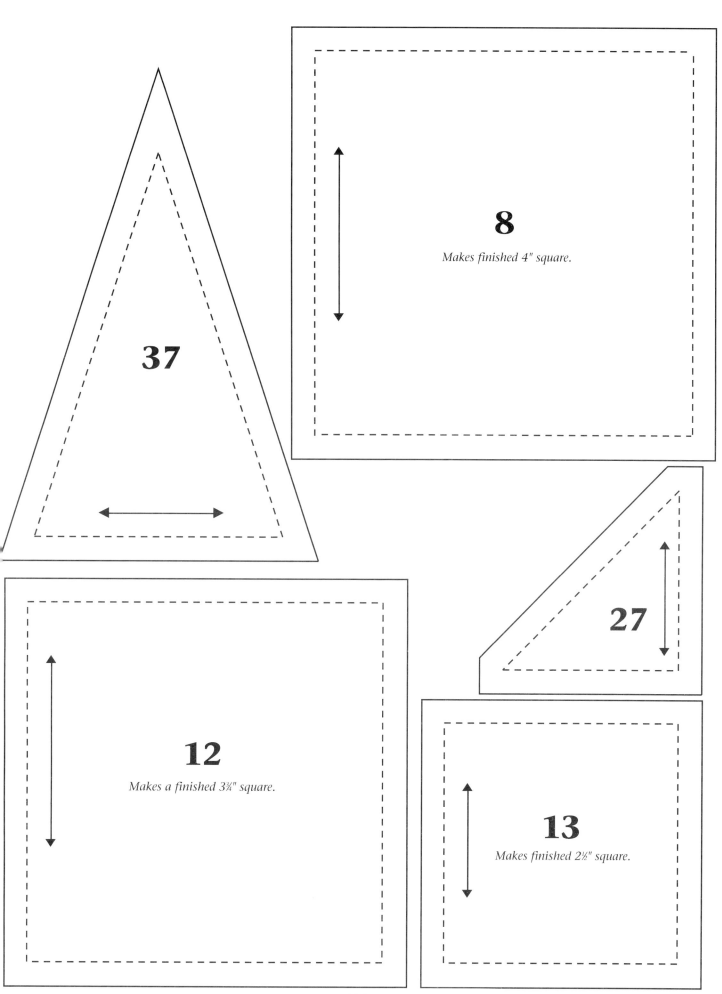

37

8

Makes finished 4" square.

27

12

Makes a finished 3¾" square.

13

Makes finished 2½" square.

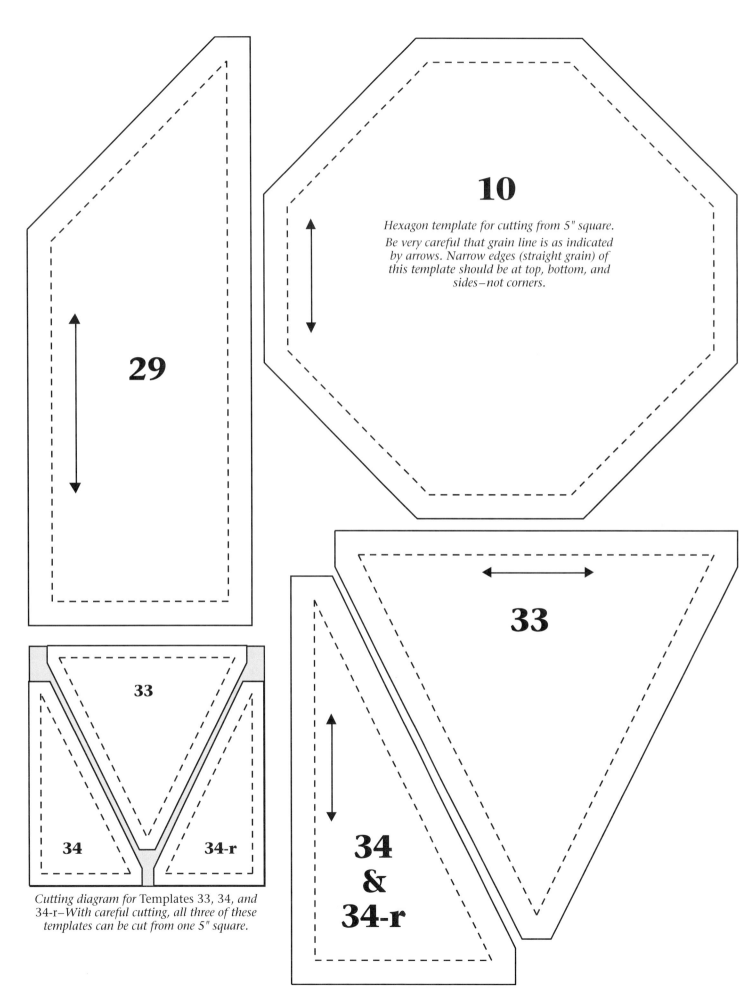

29

10

Hexagon template for cutting from 5" square.
Be very careful that grain line is as indicated
by arrows. Narrow edges (straight grain) of
this template should be at top, bottom, and
sides–not corners.

33

33

34   34-r

Cutting diagram for Templates 33, 34, and
34-r–With careful cutting, all three of these
templates can be cut from one 5" square.

34
&
34-r

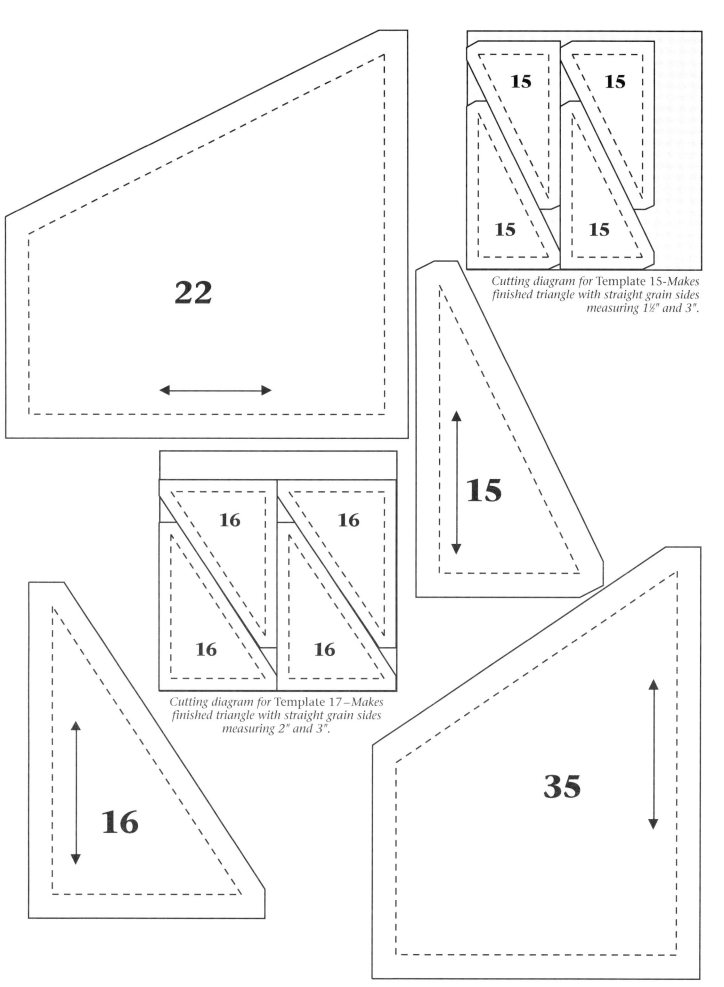

22

15
15

Cutting diagram for Template 15-Makes finished triangle with straight grain sides measuring 1½" and 3".

15
15

15

16
16

16
16

Cutting diagram for Template 17–Makes finished triangle with straight grain sides measuring 2" and 3".

16

35

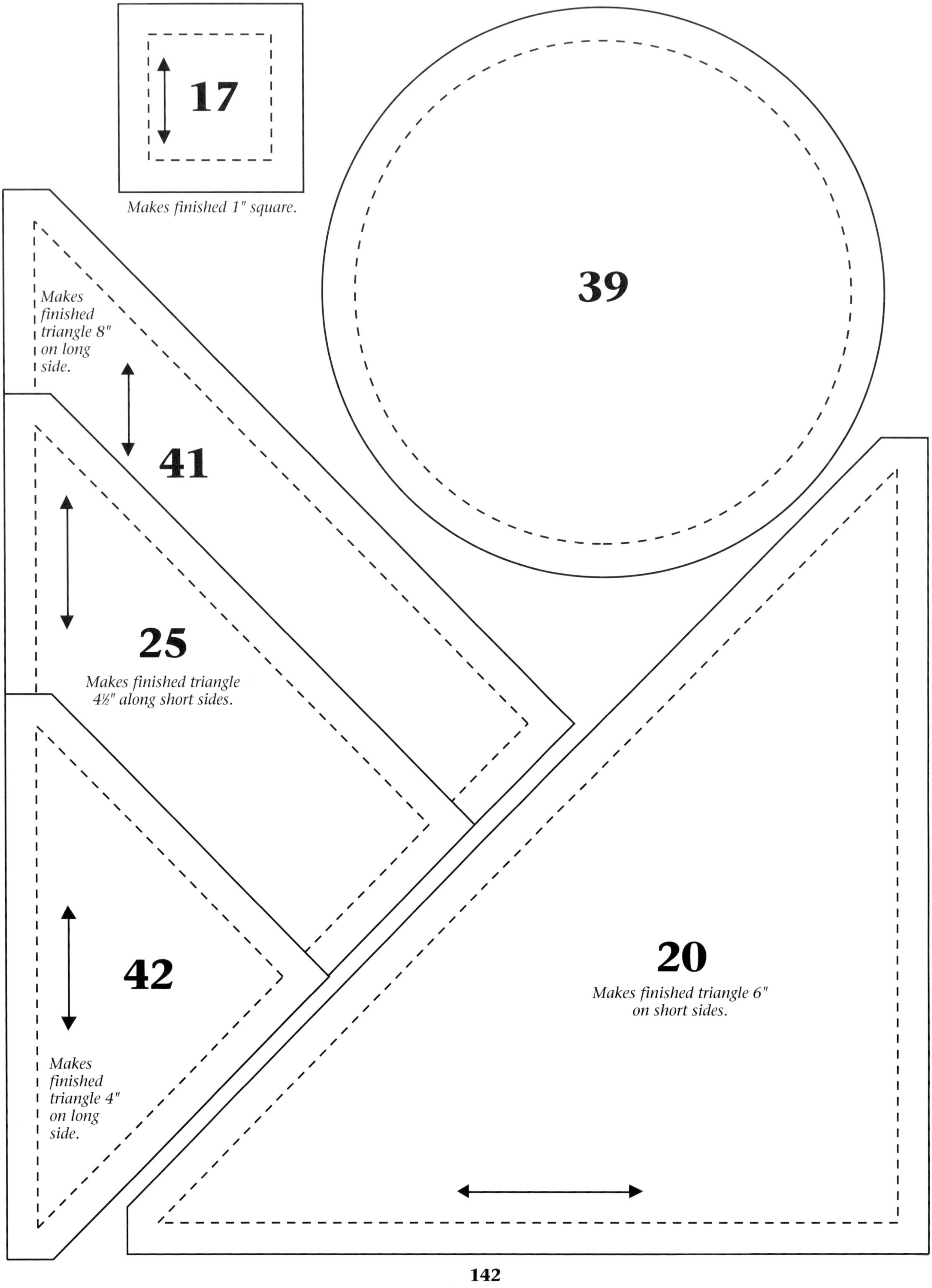

17

Makes finished 1" square.

39

Makes finished triangle 8" on long side.

41

25

Makes finished triangle 4½" along short sides.

42

Makes finished triangle 4" on long side.

20

Makes finished triangle 6" on short sides.

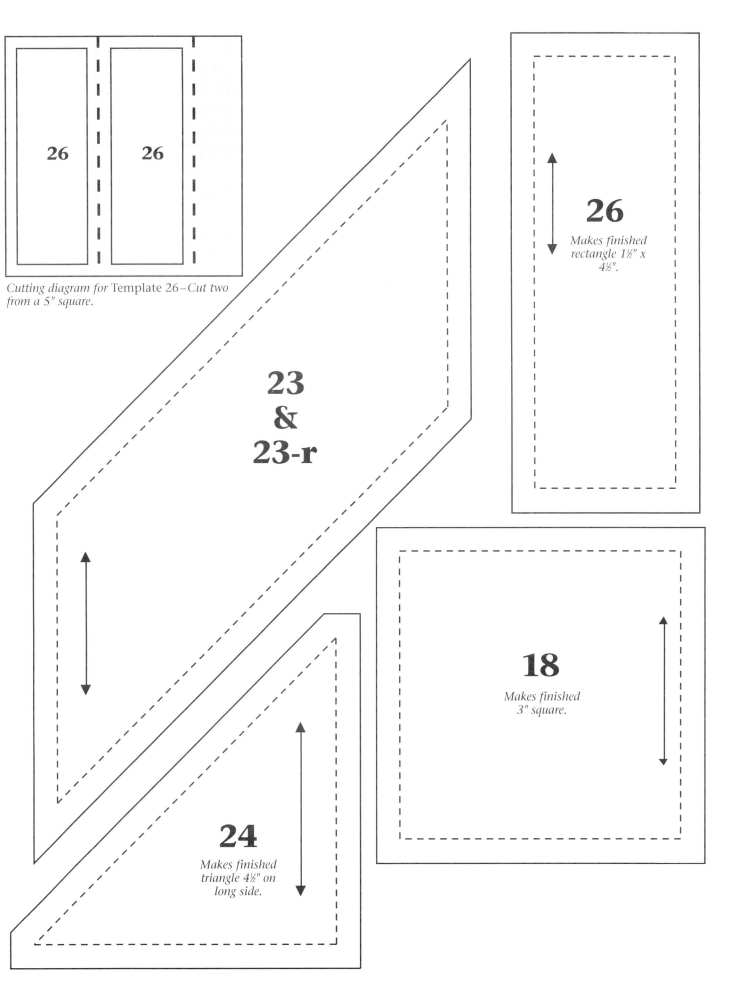

26 26

Cutting diagram for Template 26–Cut two from a 5" square.

26

Makes finished rectangle 1½" x 4½".

23 & 23-r

18

Makes finished 3" square.

24

Makes finished triangle 4½" on long side.

31

Makes finished rectangle 2" x 4".

43

Makes finished rectangle 2" x 6".

30

Makes finished rectangle 1⅞" x 5⅝".

40

21

28

Makes finished square 1⅞" x 1⅞".